THE

TUDOR

KINGS AND QUEENS

THE
TUDOR
KINGS AND QUEENS

THE DYNASTY THAT FORGED A NATION

ALEX WOOLF

ARCTURUS

ARCTURUS

This edition published in 2017 by Arcturus Publishing Limited
26/27 Bickels Yard, 151–153 Bermondsey Street,
London SE1 3HA

ISBN: 978-1-78428-252-3
DA004671UK

Printed in China

Contents

PART I: HENRY VII

Chapter 1: Founding A Dynasty 7

Chapter 2: Administering A Kingdom 17

Chapter 3: Insurrections 23

Chapter 4: Foreign Policy and Legacy 29

PART II: HENRY VIII:
EARLY REIGN: 1509–27

Chapter 5: From Prince to King 37

Chapter 6: Foreign Affairs 45

Chapter 7: Domestic Affairs 52

PART III: HENRY VIII:
LATE REIGN: 1527–47

Chapter 8: The King's Great Matter 59

Chapter 9: The Break with Rome 66

Chapter 10: The Dissolution 74
of the Monasteries

Chapter 11: Court Manoeuvres 84

PART IV: EDWARD VI (1547–53)
AND MARY I (1553–58)

Chapter 12: The Lord Protector   95
Chapter 13: The Duke of Northumberland   103
Chapter 14: Queen Mary I   112

PART V: ELIZABETH I:
EARLY REIGN (1558–81)

Chapter 15: Domestic Policies   125
Chapter 16: Foreign Policy   134
    and the Marriage Question
Chapter 17: Mary, Queen of Scots   142

PART VI: ELIZABETH I:
LATE REIGN (1581–1603)

Chapter 18: The Babington Plot   151
Chapter 19: Foreign Affairs   159
Chapter 20: Troubled Years   173

EPILOGUE   185
INDEX   187

PART I: HENRY VII

CHAPTER ONE

Founding a Dynasty

W hen King Henry VII, the first Tudor monarch, was crowned at Westminster Abbey on 30 October 1485, it marked the beginning of more than a century of Tudor rule. The Tudors were an extraordinary dynasty under whose leadership England would be transformed from a minor medieval kingdom on the margins of Europe to a major player on the world stage.

The dynasty ended in 1603 with the death of Henry's granddaughter Elizabeth I. By that time, the country had changed almost beyond recognition. The England of 1485 had been a place of instability where rival nobles would fight each other for power. By 1603, England boasted a strong central government, powerful enough to put down any rebellion. It had undergone a religious reformation, swapping Roman Catholicism for Protestantism with the monarch at the head of a new, independent Anglican Church. By the time of Elizabeth's death, England had flourishing trade links with Europe,

Henry VII's claim to the English throne was not strong: he was a descendant of John of Gaunt, via his mother and a father whose birth had to be declared legitimate by Parliament.

Asia and the New World, and had become a renowned centre of art and culture.

Arguably, many of these changes might never have

come about – or would have occurred in very different ways – were it not for the personalities and actions of this remarkable family of monarchs. Two of them – Henry VIII and Elizabeth I – were among the most famous and influential people ever to sit on the English throne. And yet it is very easy to imagine a world in which the Tudor era never happened. After all, Henry VII's accession was far from inevitable, and his claim to the throne tenuous to say the least....

THE WARS OF THE ROSES

To understand how Henry came to be king, we must first look at the situation in England at the time he took power. During this period, the English crown was being fought over by two great noble families, the houses of York and Lancaster. Both traced their ancestry to the Plantagenet King Edward III (reigned 1327–77), and both felt that they were his rightful heirs. This period of unrest is known as the Wars of the Roses because each house chose a rose as its symbol – the Lancastrians sported a red rose, the Yorkists a white one.

The Lancastrians were descended from the first Duke of Lancaster, John of Gaunt (1340–99), a son of Edward III. They held the throne of England for 72 years, through the reigns of Henry IV, Henry V and Henry VI. But the last of these, Henry VI (1421–71), was a weak king, and during his unstable reign the Yorkists attempted to seize power, sparking the Wars of the Roses.

In 1471, after 16 years of fighting, the House of York won a decisive victory. Both Henry VI and his son Edward were killed shortly after the battle, ending the Lancastrian line of succession. Edward, Duke of York, was crowned King Edward IV (for the second time – he'd also been king from 1461 to 1470), and it seemed that the Wars of the Roses had finally been won by the Yorkists.

Except that the Lancastrian line was not quite extinguished. All the legitimate descendants of John of Gaunt had died out or been killed, but the Lancastrian patriarch had also had quite a few children born out of wedlock, and a descendant of one of these illegitimate offspring now turned up on the scene as the new Lancastrian claimant. That man was Henry Tudor.

Meanwhile, the Yorkists were having trouble establishing a royal dynasty. In 1483, Edward IV unexpectedly died. Just 86 days later, his son, 13-year-old Edward V, mysteriously disappeared from the Tower of London, along with his younger brother, Richard of Shrewsbury, Duke of York. Edward V was succeeded by his uncle Richard. Richard III proved an unpopular ruler, and support among the nobility began shifting back towards the Lancastrians – which meant Henry Tudor, despite his illegitimate line of descent. Henry raised an army in France and invaded in 1485, defeating Richard at the Battle of Bosworth Field. Richard was killed in the battle, and Henry Tudor was shortly thereafter crowned King Henry VII.

By marrying Elizabeth of York, Henry managed to unite the two rival houses and bring the Wars of the Roses to an end. However, the Yorkist challenge would flicker on for a while longer in the form of a number of rebellions. The final pitched battle of the wars was fought in 1487, when Henry's army defeated the Yorkist pretender Lambert Simnel.

THE BASIS OF HENRY'S CLAIM

Henry's mother was Margaret Beaufort, granddaughter of John Beaufort, son of John of Gaunt and his mistress Katherine Swynford. Thus, Henry's claim to the throne was especially tenuous, for it was not only through illegitimate descent, but also through a woman – Margaret. Moreover, in 1407, King Henry IV decreed that the descendants of Gaunt and Swynford were ineligible for the throne, further weakening Henry Tudor's claim.

However, Henry did have another royal connection, through his father, Edmund Tudor, 1st Earl of Richmond. Edmund's father was Owen Tudor. Originally from Anglesey in Wales, Owen had been a courtier of King Henry V. After the King died, Owen became the lover, and possibly husband, of his widow, Catherine of Valois. They had several children together, including Edmund.

Henry could also point to his Welsh ancestry. The Tudors were an old Anglesey family that claimed descent from Cadwaladr, a legendary seventh-century king. This would help Henry attract support during his army's march through Wales on the way to the Battle of Bosworth Field.

Although Henry owed much to his paternal heritage, he never met his father. While Margaret Beaufort was pregnant, her husband Edmund was in South Wales, fighting for Henry VI against the Yorkists. He was captured and imprisoned in Carmarthen Castle, and died there, three months before his son was born.

EARLY LIFE

Henry Tudor was born on 28 January 1457 at Pembroke Castle in Wales. His mother Margaret was just 13 years old at the time, and already a widow. At first they were looked after by Jasper Tudor, Earl of Pembroke and younger brother of Edmund. But Jasper was forced to

Henry was born in Wales at Pembroke Castle, beside the River Cleddau.

flee abroad in 1461 when the Yorkist King Edward IV took power, and care of Henry and his mother was entrusted to the Yorkist William Herbert. During a brief resurgence of Lancastrian fortunes (1469–71), Jasper Tudor returned and Henry was brought to the court of Henry VI. But when Edward IV regained the throne in 1471, Henry, Jasper, Margaret and the other Lancastrians fled to Brittany, where they would remain for 12 years.

In 1483, the now adult Henry believed his time had come: Edward IV had died; his son and heir, Edward V, had disappeared, together with his younger brother; and the unpopular Richard III had seized the throne. Henry raised an army of Bretons, planning to time his invasion to coincide with an uprising of his supporters in England. However, a storm separated Henry from the main body of his fleet and the uprising failed, forcing Henry to return to Brittany. Richard III, alarmed by the attempted invasion, pressured the Bretons to hand Henry over to him. Before they could do so, Henry escaped across the border to France.

From this time onwards, Henry's fortunes rapidly improved. Along with his Lancastrian followers, he gained the support of a number of disaffected Yorkists who had been angered by Richard's policies. In 1485, Henry persuaded the King of France to supply him with troops and equipment for a second invasion. He landed in Mill Bay, Pembrokeshire, close to his birthplace, and marched from there to England, gathering supporters as he went. Henry knew that his best chance lay in engaging Richard's forces early, as the Yorkists had reinforcements in Nottingham and Leicester that would shortly be joining their main army.

The two armies met at Bosworth Field in Leicestershire on 22 August. Despite being outnumbered, Henry's forces won a decisive victory. They were helped by the fact that several of Richard's key allies defected to the Lancastrian side during the course of the battle. However, the crucial moment came when Richard was killed. Had he survived the battle, it may have gone down as just another skirmish in an ongoing civil war. Richard's death is one of the main reasons why Bosworth Field is remembered as a major turning point in British history.

SECURING POWER

That is not to say that Henry's victory was complete. His triumph at Bosworth may have won him the crown by right of conquest, but it was far from certain that he would keep it. To secure his rule, and restore peace and order to his kingdom, Henry would have to tread very carefully.

His first task was to remove any rival royal claimants. While still in Leicestershire, he ordered the imprisonment of 10-year-old Edward, Earl of Warwick, nephew of Edward IV, thus preventing him from becoming a rallying point for Yorkist rebels.

Next, Henry moved to establish his legitimacy as

Richard III and the Earl of Richmond at the Battle of Bosworth, 22 August 1485.

sovereign. He had himself crowned on 30 October 1485, a week before Parliament was due to meet. The timing was deliberate, as it ensured Parliament had no chance to claim that Henry's accession had depended on its consent. Instead, when Parliament met, it was required only to pass a statute establishing that the crown should 'rest and abide in the most royal person of our now sovereign lord King Henry VII and in the heirs of his body'.

This gave some legal substance to Henry's rule. He further solidified his position in the hearts and minds of many of his former enemies by taking as his wife Elizabeth of York, eldest child of the late King Edward IV. With this marriage, which took place on 18 January 1485, the two warring houses were unified, and any children the couple had would have strong claims to the throne. Henry symbolically linked the two houses with a new national emblem, the Tudor rose, which combined the white rose of York with the red rose of Lancaster.

SHAKESPEARE'S HENRY TUDOR

William Shakespeare, writing during the reign of Henry Tudor's granddaughter Elizabeth I, took care to glorify Henry and the dynasty he would found. His play *King Richard the Third* ends on the battlefield of Bosworth with the death of Richard and the crowning of Henry. In Henry's final speech, he looks forward to a golden time of peace and prosperity under his heirs:

> *England hath long been mad, and scarred herself;*
> *The brother blindly shed the brother's blood;*
> *The father rashly slaughtered his own son;*
> *The son, compelled, been butcher to the sire;*
> *All that divided York and Lancaster,*
> *United in their dire division.*
> *O, now let Richmond and Elizabeth,*
> *The true succeeders of each royal house,*
> *By God's fair ordinance conjoin together,*
> *And let their heirs, God, if his will be so,*
> *Enrich the time to come with smooth-faced peace,*
> *With smiling plenty, and fair prosperous days.*

King Richard the Third, Act V, Scene 5

CHAPTER TWO

Administering a Kingdom

Throughout his reign, Henry VII was driven by a determination to make his position, and that of his heirs, secure. This desire lay at the heart of all his policies. A key part of his strategy for survival involved the restoration of royal authority, which had become badly eroded during the Wars of the Roses. A system had arisen during this period known as 'bastard feudalism', in which powerful nobles acquired their own private armies made up of retainers – servants wearing their lords' uniforms – loyal to their lord, not the king.

TAMING THE NOBLES

Henry used a policy of divide and rule to bring the nobles to heel. To those who showed him loyalty he offered lands and titles. For example, Lord Stanley, his stepfather, was given Lancashire and Cheshire, and his uncle Jasper was made Duke of Bedford. Even members of the York family were rewarded if they proved themselves trustworthy. For instance, Thomas Howard, Earl of Surrey, was made Lord Treasurer in 1501.

Others whom he perceived as threats were reined in through the force of law. In 1487, Henry passed laws against 'livery' (the practice by nobles of allowing their servants to wear their badges and emblems) and 'maintenance' (the practice of retaining private armies). Nobles who broke these laws were forced to pay fines.

JUSTICES OF THE PEACE

Henry enforced his laws and extended royal power into the shires by establishing a system of Justices of the Peace. These officials were appointed in every shire of the country, their chief responsibility being to ensure that the law was obeyed in their locality. Justices of the Peace only served for a year at a time, so were unlikely to become powerful in their own right. They were unpaid, allowing Henry to save a great deal of money. Yet the positions were eagerly filled by members of the gentry who saw it as a way of obtaining influence and prestige in their local area, often at the expense of the nobles.

THE ROYAL COUNCIL

At the heart of Henry's administration lay the Royal Council, an inner circle of loyal nobles and clerics who acted as advisors to the king. These included Jasper Tudor and John de Vere, Earl of Oxford. Among the most powerful to serve on the council were John Moreton, the Lord Chancellor and later Archbishop of Canterbury, and Richard Fox, the King's Secretary and Bishop of Winchester.

During the years of Henry's reign, a total of 227 people served on the Royal Council. However, there were never more than 150 serving at any one time, and the average attendance at meetings was around 40. The King also made use of educated professionals, such as lawyers and clerks, to assist with the work of the Royal Council. Because their skills were so valuable to him, he did not care much what class they came from.

THE STAR CHAMBER

Henry wanted to ensure that the common-law courts around the country weren't being manipulated by locally powerful nobles. So he established the Star Chamber (named for the star pattern on the ceiling of the room at Westminster Palace where its meetings were held). This was a supervisory court under the king's direct control, which would oversee the operations and verdicts of the lower courts, hear cases on appeal and make sure the law was being fairly enforced.

This wasn't without precedent. Medieval kings had long presided over courts composed of their Privy Councillors. However, under Henry, the Star Chamber was turned into a separate judicial body, distinct from the Royal Council. Sessions of the Star Chamber were held in secret before a panel of judges. There were no witnesses, and evidence was presented in writing. This allowed the Star Chamber to develop, in time, into a powerful and greatly feared instrument of royal power.

PARLIAMENT

The institution of Parliament had existed since Anglo-Saxon times. It originated because Anglo-Saxon kings realized they couldn't govern their territories without the support of powerful nobles living in those lands. They would call these nobles together from time to time to gain approval for decisions, particularly regarding taxation. After the Norman Conquest of 1066, Parliament evolved into a legislative assembly made up of two chambers: the Lords (composed of earls, barons, bishops and abbots) and the Commons (composed of local representatives from the towns and shires, including knights and burgesses).

Over time, Parliament gradually grew in power. Under Edward I (1272–1307) it became an accepted custom that the king needed the consent of Parliament before he could raise new taxes. As monarchs needed lots of money to wage their wars, they began to summon Parliament on a regular basis – usually at least once a year. Between 1327 and 1485 there were only 42 years in which Parliament did not meet.

Henry VII broke with this tradition. He viewed Parliament as a threat to his power and did not want to become dependent on it for money as previous monarchs had, so he summoned it as infrequently as possible. In fact, during Henry's 24-year reign, Parliament met on only seven occasions, and five of these were between 1485 and 1495 when he was still establishing himself. Henry could afford not to call Parliament too often because, unlike his predecessors, his policy was to avoid expensive wars.

When he did call Parliament, Henry used it to enact laws that reinforced his position, establishing and extending royal power. For example, some 10 per cent of all laws passed were concerned with the responsibilities of justices of the peace and their control in the shires. If any Member of Parliament tried to oppose the King, he risked being condemned by an act of attainder, allowing him to be punished, even executed, without trial. Parliament therefore quickly became a rubber stamp for Henry.

FINANCES

Henry inherited a royal treasury that was, after 30 years of civil war, almost bankrupt. Yet by the time he died, thanks to his skilful financial management, he was able to bequeath a considerable fortune to his heir. Wisely, he kept a stable team of financial advisors. Except for a few months in 1485, just two men held the office of Lord High Treasurer during Henry's reign, Lord Dynham and Thomas Howard, Earl of Surrey.

Henry's tax collectors were feared for their ruthlessness and efficiency. His Chancellor, Archbishop John Morton, devised a brilliant method of ensuring payment of taxes, known as Morton's Fork. By this principle, if a noble spent little, it must be assumed that he had saved much, and so could afford to pay higher taxes. Conversely, if he spent a lot, he was obviously wealthy, and so he could also afford to pay higher taxes. By this catch-22 logic, no noble could escape Henry's tax levies.

Early in his reign, Henry substantially increased the royal lands (and thereby the revenues from rents) by having Parliament backdate his reign to the day before the Battle of Bosworth Field. By this device he turned all those who fought against him at the battle into traitors, enabling him to claim their estates as forfeit for treason. Through efficient administration of his royal lands, Henry increased their value, and by the end of his reign they were yielding him around £35,000 per annum.

Another important source of income for Henry was customs revenue from foreign trade. After persuading his first Parliament to grant him customs revenue for the whole of his life, Henry went about encouraging trade through international diplomacy, substantially increasing customs yield. Finally, by expanding the reach and effectiveness of his courts, Henry could rely on a steady income from the 'profits of justice' – in other words, fines.

All these policies led to a rise in royal income from an average of £52,000 per annum in 1485 to £142,000 per annum by 1509.

CHAPTER THREE

Insurrections

Following his victory at Bosworth Field, Henry acted quickly to remove all possible Yorkist rivals to the throne. He took the most prominent of these, Elizabeth of York, as his wife, then married off three of Elizabeth's younger sisters to loyal supporters (the fourth sister became a nun). Elizabeth's cousin, the child Edward, Earl of Warwick, was imprisoned in the Tower of London, and the de la Pole brothers (nephews of Edward IV and Richard III) all swore loyalty to Henry after the battle. Therefore, the main threat to Henry did not come from the Yorkists themselves, but from impostors.

LAMBERT SIMNEL

The first of these impostors was a boy called Lambert Simnel. Born in Oxford in around 1477 in humble circumstances, Simnel led a quiet life until the age of 10, when he was taken on as a pupil by a priest named Richard Simon. Simon noticed a startling resemblance between Simnel and the missing sons of Edward IV – Edward V and Richard of Shrewsbury, Duke of York, the 'Princes in the Tower'. A staunch Yorkist, Simon realized that he could use Simnel as the figurehead for an already-planned rebellion against Henry VII, so he set about training the boy in courtly manners.

When Simon heard that Edward, Earl of Warwick, had died during his imprisonment in the Tower of London, he changed his plans. Simnel was closer in age to Warwick and so would be more credible in that role. Simon spread a rumour that Warwick had escaped from the Tower and that he was acting as his guardian. Then he took Simnel to Ireland, where there was still some support for the Yorkist cause, and presented him to the Earl of Kildare. The earl accepted the story, and Simnel was paraded through the streets of Dublin and crowned King Edward VI. Kildare raised an army of Irish soldiers, soon supplemented by 2,000 Flemish mercenaries gathered by the Earl of Lincoln and Warwick's aunt, Margaret of York.

Simnel's Flemish-Irish army landed on Piel Island in Lancashire on 5 June 1487. It attracted a few English supporters, but most of the local nobility failed to join it. Henry's army met the insurgents at Stoke on 16 June. The battle, which is considered the final clash of the Wars of the Roses, was actually a closer-run thing than Bosworth Field and resulted in much higher casualties. The result, however, was a crushing victory for Henry. Almost all the leading Yorkists, including the Earl of Lincoln, were killed.

Henry showed remarkable mercy to the surviving rebels. He pardoned the Earl of Kildare and other Irish supporters of the rebellion, including the Bishop of Meath, who had presided over Simnel's 'coronation'. Richard Simon was imprisoned but not executed. As for Simnel himself, Henry realized that he was just a Yorkist puppet and not deserving of punishment. So he gave him a job in the royal kitchens as a turnspit, later promoting him to falconer.

PERKIN WARBECK

Another pretender to the English throne emerged in the 1490s. Perkin Warbeck is a mysterious figure. Much of what we know about his life is based on a confession he made in 1497, which may or may not be true. According to this, he was born in about 1474 in the city of Tournai (in what is now Belgium) to a Flemish bureaucrat named John Osbeck. At the age of 10, Warbeck travelled with his mother to the Netherlands, where he found employment as a merchant's assistant.

Warbeck first laid claim to the English throne at the court of Burgundy in 1490, when he was about 16. He announced that he was Richard of Shrewsbury, Duke of York, the younger son of Edward IV, and explained that his brother Edward V had been murdered but the killers had spared him because of his age and 'innocence' so long as he promised not to reveal his true identity for 'a certain number of years'. After finding little support for his claims in Ireland or at the court of the King of France, Warbeck received the blessing of Margaret of York, based in Burgundy, who proclaimed him her nephew (whether she believed it or not). He was tutored in the ways of court life and was also welcomed by other European monarchs as 'King Richard IV of England'.

With Margaret's help, Warbeck raised a small army and launched an invasion, landing at Deal in Kent on 3 July 1495. His army was crushed before Warbeck even made it to shore, and the pretender fled to Ireland. Here he was welcomed by the Earl of Desmond, with whose help he laid siege to Waterford. The city held out, and Warbeck was forced, once again, to flee, this time to Scotland. King James IV of Scotland spied an opportunity and decided to use Warbeck in his own struggles with England. In September 1496, James IV and Warbeck's army crossed the River Tweed into England. But the hoped-for support from Northumberland failed to appear, and when an English army approached from Newcastle, the Scots retreated, having only penetrated six and a half kilometres (four miles).

Tiring of Warbeck, James returned him to Ireland in July 1497. The pretender made a second attempt to capture Waterford, but was chased away by some English warships. In September 1497, the tenacious Warbeck landed in Whitesand Bay, Cornwall, this time hoping to rally local support for his cause. The Cornish people had rebelled just three months earlier and many of them

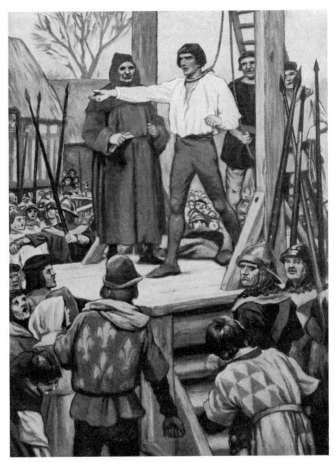

Perkin Warbeck, one of the pretenders to the throne, at his hanging in 1499.

welcomed Warbeck, proclaiming him king on Bodmin Moor. Warbeck raised a 6,000-strong Cornish army and marched on Taunton, but when he heard that an English army was approaching from Glastonbury, he panicked and deserted his men.

He was captured at Beaulieu Abbey in Hampshire and imprisoned in the Tower of London. As with Simnel before him, Warbeck was treated well by Henry. Once he had confessed to being an impostor, he was allowed to attend Henry's court and his royal banquets, although kept under guard at all times. In March 1499, Warbeck tried to escape, but was quickly recaptured and imprisoned in the Tower. After a second escape attempt in November 1499, he was hanged at Tyburn in London.

THE LAST PRETENDER

Following the death of the Earl of Warwick, Edmund de la Pole, Earl of Suffolk, assumed the mantle of chief royal pretender. He was the brother of the Earl of Lincoln, who had died at the Battle of Stoke, and was resentful towards the King for forbidding him from inheriting his dead father's dukedom. In 1501, Suffolk journeyed with his brother Richard to the court of the Holy Roman Emperor, Maximilian I, and began to gather support for an invasion. Hearing of this, Henry imprisoned all of Suffolk's relations and confiscated their lands. In 1506, Henry negotiated with the Duke of Burgundy for Suffolk's return to England, on condition that he would not be put to death. Henry was true to his word and spared Suffolk's life, but he spent the rest of his days in the Tower of London. He was executed in 1513 on the orders of Henry VIII.

CHAPTER FOUR

Foreign Policy and Legacy

Henry VII was not ambitious in foreign affairs. He had no wish to conquer new lands or be an international power broker. His main aims were to have his dynasty recognized by foreign rulers, and to secure peace and prosperity for his kingdom. And in these modest ambitions, he was reasonably successful, achieving his goals, more often than not, through a skilful mixture of diplomacy, dynastic marriages and trade agreements, rather than on the battlefield.

FRANCE

Henry had no interest in trying to regain the French territories lost during the reigns of his predecessors and at first he pursued a policy of peaceful coexistence with his powerful neighbour. However, in 1487, France tried to annexe the independent Duchy of Brittany. The Bretons had sheltered Henry during his long exile as a boy, so he may have felt personally obliged to help them – but in doing so, he also acted from pragmatic motives: Brittany was an important trading partner; also, he did not relish the idea of France occupying the entire southern coast of the English Channel, threatening English shipping. So Henry agreed to send troops to Brittany. After a series of battles, the Bretons and their English allies were defeated, and in 1491 France took control of Brittany.

Uncharacteristically, Henry now decided to pursue a more aggressive course of action, invading northern France in October 1492 and laying siege to Boulogne. Distracted by her own expansionist moves in northern Italy, France did not want a war and decided to come to a deal. The result was the Treaty of Étaples (November 1492). Under its terms, the King of France, Charles VIII, agreed not to give shelter to pretenders to the English throne (this was during the era of Perkin Warbeck) and to pay Henry 50,000 crowns a year, greatly swelling the King's coffers. In return, Henry agreed to accept French control of Brittany. The treaty held, and England and France remained at peace for the rest of Henry's reign.

SCOTLAND

Apart from France, England's other traditional enemy was Scotland. Keen to secure his northern border, Henry signed a three-year truce with the Scots in 1486. The situation changed in 1488 when James III of Scotland was killed and his son came to the throne as James IV. Henry was not too concerned – the new king was only

15 and did not appear to offer a threat. Tensions mounted, however, when James gave support to the pretender Perkin Warbeck. Although the Warbeck rebellion failed, it made Henry realize how vulnerable the border was and he began to pursue a treaty with Scotland. In 1497, the Truce of Ayton was signed.

Border raids continued, however, as did mistrust between the kingdoms, and the situation was only resolved with the signing of the Treaty of Perpetual Peace in 1502 – the first peace treaty between the two nations since 1328. As part of the treaty, it was agreed that James IV should marry Henry's daughter, Margaret Tudor. The peace held for just 11 years, but the consequences of the treaty lasted much longer. Thanks to the marriage that sealed it, the great-grandson of James IV and Margaret would succeed to the English throne in 1603 (after the last Tudor, Elizabeth I, died), uniting the two kingdoms under a single monarch.

SPAIN

Early in his reign, Henry saw that an alliance with Spain would offer him a number of advantages. This powerful new kingdom (formed in 1479 with the joining of Aragon and Castile) could enable him to keep France in check, as well as help him secure greater English trade in the Mediterranean. A formal treaty with Spain would also give his insecure kingship some much-needed legitimacy. In 1489, Henry signed the Treaty of Medina del Campo with Spain's joint rulers, Ferdinand II and Isabella I. Under its terms, Henry's three-year-old son Arthur was betrothed to the Spanish sovereigns' equally young daughter, Catherine of Aragon.

The treaty proved a great success for Henry, both diplomatically and financially: when Catherine finally wed Arthur, in November 1501, she brought with her a dowry of 100,000 crowns. Sadly, Arthur died just five months later. This was a personal tragedy for Henry and also a severe blow to the Spanish alliance. However, Henry was able to secure Ferdinand and Isabella's blessing for Catherine to marry his second son, the future King Henry VIII.

OTHER FOREIGN POLICY ACHIEVEMENTS

In his attempts to secure his dynasty and provide prosperity for his realm, Henry also achieved the following:

- He persuaded Pope Innocent VIII to declare him the rightful holder of the English crown (1486).
- He renewed a treaty with the Holy Roman Emperor Maximilian I (1487).
- He made a treaty with Denmark to secure fishing rights for English fishermen in Icelandic waters (1489).
- He formed an agreement with the Italian city of Florence for the sale of English wool (1490).
- He signed the *Magnus Intercursus* (Great Intercourse)

agreement with the Netherlands, removing taxation on English textile exports.

- He financed the voyages of John Cabot into the North Atlantic, resulting in the discovery of rich new fishing grounds (1497–9).

THE MAN AND HIS LEGACY

Unlike his son, Henry VIII, or granddaughter, Elizabeth I, the first Tudor king does not appear to have been very charismatic. It doesn't help that little is known about him. Although well educated, Henry rarely put his thoughts down on paper, so he appears to us fairly opaque. One of the best descriptions we have of him was by the Italian scholar Polydore Vergil:

His body was slender, but well built and strong; his height above average. His appearance was remarkably attractive and his face cheerful, especially when speaking; his eyes were small and blue, his teeth few, poor and blackish; his hair was thin and white; his complexion sallow. His spirit was distinguished, wise and prudent; his mind was brave and resolute, and never, even at moments of greatest danger, deserted him. He had a most pertinacious memory. Withal he was not devoid of scholarship. In government, he was shrewd and prudent, so that no one dared to get the better of him through deceit and guile.

Because of the way Henry carefully managed his money, he gained a reputation as a miser. Yet he could be very generous with his spending. Historical documents record that he spent money on a children's choir, an impressive stable of horses, a private zoo, dancers, musicians and fine banquets.

Henry has been described by some of his biographers as cold-hearted, and it is true that he was not generally given to extravagant displays of emotion. Yet he surprised his courtiers with his intense grief on the death of his son Arthur, and when his wife Elizabeth died in childbirth in 1503 he fell into a deep depression and, according to one chronicler, 'privily departed to a solitary place and would no man should resort unto him'.

Henry died of tuberculosis at Richmond Palace on 21 April 1509 and was buried at Westminster Abbey in a chapel alongside his wife Elizabeth. In his funeral oration, John Fisher, Bishop of Rochester, said of the King:

> *His politic wisdom in government was singular; his reason pithy and substantial, his memory fresh and holding, his experience notable, his counsels fortunate and taken with wise deliberation, his speech gracious in diverse languages ... his dealings in time of peril and dangers was cold and sober with great hardiness.*

Henry left his kingdom strong, at peace and, by past standards, wealthy. His sober and efficient statesmanship had enhanced England's standing among the major European powers. At home, he had greatly strengthened the position of the monarchy in relation to the nobility, creating a powerful centralized administration. In so doing, he had laid the foundations for a successful dynasty.

PART II: HENRY VIII: EARLY REIGN: 1509–27

CHAPTER FIVE

From Prince to King

The new king, Henry VIII, was crowned on 24 June 1509. The streets were hung with tapestries and cloth-of-gold, and the handsome young monarch wore a golden coat with a collar of rubies and a red velvet, ermine-trimmed robe. People lined the streets to cheer Henry and his queen, Catherine of Aragon, as they made their way from the Palace of Westminster to Westminster Abbey for the ceremony. Henry was very popular with the crowds, and most agreed that he would make a fine king. He was tall, with an athletic physique, and was known to be an accomplished sportsman and an able scholar. He loved art, music and culture, as well as gambling, hunting and jousting. Unlike his dour father, the young Henry VIII appeared to have a real zest for life. A Venetian visitor wrote of the youthful king: 'His majesty is the handsomest potentate I ever set eyes on,' with a face so delicate 'that it would become a pretty woman'. Another commentator rhapsodized that 'Nature could not have done more for him. He is much handsomer than the King of France, very fair and his whole frame admirably proportioned.'

Henry VIII, a second son who became his father's heir only on the death of his older brother.

The second son

Prince Henry was born at the Palace of Placentia at Greenwich on 28 June 1491, the third child of Henry VII and Elizabeth of York. Just three of his six siblings survived infancy: Arthur (1486–1502), Margaret (1489–1541) and Mary (1496–1533). As a toddler, Henry was precocious, noted for his energy and temper. His elder brother Arthur, as heir to the throne, was the main focus of his father's attention, and it was left to Henry's grandmother, Margaret Beaufort, to supervise his early education.

As the second son, Henry was groomed for a senior role in the Church, probably Archbishop of Canterbury, and he was given a first-rate education from the foremost tutors of the day. The focus of his education was theology, but he was also taught Latin, French, grammar, history, rhetoric, logic, philosophy, arithmetic, literature, geometry, music, astronomy, navigation and cartography. In addition to academic subjects, Henry was also given instruction in riding, jousting, tennis, archery, hunting and dancing.

He showed effortless prowess in both sport and study, and even tried his hand at composing music. Spoiled by his mother and grandmother, fawned on by friends and surrounded by servants ready to indulge his every whim, Henry enjoyed an idyllic childhood. All that changed when his elder brother Arthur died of the 'sweating sickness'. Suddenly, aged 10, Henry was heir to the throne and his life became very different indeed.

HEIR APPARENT

Henry's grief-stricken father, determined that his remaining son should survive to succeed him, banned the young Henry from practising dangerous sports and kept him secluded in his apartments where he was allowed only the company of tutors, servants and guards. Accounts suggest a stormy relationship between father and son. Reginald Pole, Prince Henry's cousin, said that the King had 'no affection' for his son, and in one reported incident in 1508, they quarrelled so violently that it appeared as if the King 'sought to kill' the prince.

On 25 June 1503, when Henry was still just shy of his twelfth birthday, he was betrothed to his brother's 17-year-old widow, Catherine of Aragon. His father arranged this to avoid having to hand back Catherine's wedding dowry, as well as to maintain the alliance with Spain. Problems ensued, however, as relations between the two kingdoms deteriorated. In 1505, when Henry was 14 and old enough to wed, his father ordered him to reject the betrothal. For the next four years, Catherine was left in limbo as Henry VII dithered over returning the dowry. Despite this, the devout princess continued to believe that it was God's will that she would marry Prince Henry.

The prince may have felt similarly about Catherine, for as soon as his father died he applied for papal dispensation to marry her. This was required because canon law forbade a man to marry his brother's widow.

Catherine testified that her marriage to Arthur had never been consummated, and so – also according to canon law – was not valid. The Pope gave his blessing, and Prince Henry and Catherine were married in a private ceremony at Greenwich Church on 11 June 1509, two weeks before the groom's coronation.

THE YOUNG KING AND THE RISE OF WOLSEY

Unlike his father, Henry VIII showed little appetite for the daily grind of politics and administration. He preferred to leave affairs of state to his ministers. For the first two years, government policy was directed by his two leading ministers, Richard Fox, Bishop of Winchester and Lord Privy Seal, and William Warham, Archbishop of Canterbury. From 1511, however, power became increasingly concentrated in the hands of a man named Thomas Wolsey.

Fox and Warham had been long-time advisors to Henry VII. Conservative in their outlook, they counselled the young king to be a cautious ruler like his father. Caution was not in Henry's nature, however. He began to look for advisors who were more sympathetic with his own views. Thomas Wolsey saw his opportunity, and grabbed it.

Born in 1473 to an Ipswich cattle dealer and butcher, Wolsey had studied theology at Oxford, and in 1498 he was ordained as a priest. He was appointed Dean of Divinity at Magdalen College, Oxford, then chaplain to the Archbishop of Canterbury. Around this time, his exceptional management skills came to the attention of Henry VII, and in 1507 he was made the King's chaplain. When Henry VIII came to the throne, he appointed Wolsey as his almoner, giving him a seat on the Privy Council. Wolsey was thus able to meet with the King on a regular basis and establish a rapport with him.

By 1511, Henry was eager to go to war with France. Fox and Warham cautioned against this. Wolsey, who had also been anti-war until this point, suddenly changed his mind and started giving speeches to the Privy Council in favour of war. Fox, who had supported Wolsey during his rise, soon found himself eclipsed by him. In 1516, Fox resigned the Privy Seal. By this time, Warham had resigned as Lord Chancellor, probably under pressure from the King and Wolsey, and Henry had appointed Wolsey in his place. As Lord Chancellor, Wolsey became the King's chief advisor and easily the most powerful man in the land after Henry.

Wolsey cemented his power by destroying or winning over rivals. He was probably instrumental in the fall of influential people such as Edward Stafford, Duke of Buckingham, Henry's friend William Compton and Henry's ex-mistress, Anne Stafford, the Countess of Huntingdon. As well as being Lord Chancellor, Wolsey continued to rise within the Church, becoming Canon of Windsor in 1511, Bishop of Lincoln and then Archbishop of York in 1514, cardinal in 1515 and papal

Cardinal Wolsey, who eventually amassed so much power he became known as *alter rex* (the other king).

legate in 1518. As official representative of the Pope, he effectively became the head of the Church in England, wielding more power than the Archbishop of Canterbury.

With power came great wealth, and by 1529 he was the richest man in England after the King. He spent his money on huge building projects. Of his four main palaces, Hampton Court was the biggest and most glorious. Wolsey enjoyed an almost regal lifestyle with his own court of more than 500 people. The butcher's son from Ipswich had come to be known as *alter rex*, the 'other king'.

CHAPTER SIX

Foreign Affairs

For the first 20 years of Henry's reign, England's foreign policy was focused on extracting maximum advantage from the shifting pattern of alliances between Europe's great powers – France, Spain and the Holy Roman Empire. In 1511, Pope Julius II formed a Holy League in an attempt to thwart the ambitions of Louis XII of France, who was aiming to expand his territories in northern Italy. Henry VIII and Wolsey decided to join the Holy League, which already included Ferdinand II of Spain and the Holy Roman Emperor, Maximilian I. Henry was hoping that this would provide an opportunity to expand English territory in northern France.

WAR WITH FRANCE AND SCOTLAND

Henry sent an army to France led by Thomas Grey, Marquess of Dorset, in 1512, but the campaign was a failure. Queen Catherine and Wolsey persuaded Henry to launch a second offensive the following year. He decided to lead this army himself, and took part in the successful sieges of Thérouanne and Tournai. Then, together with Maximilian I, he beat the French at the Battle of Guinegate (16 August 1513), also known as the Battle of the Spurs.

The King of France, Louis XII, appealed to King James IV of Scotland for assistance. James, despite being married to Henry's sister, decided to honour the 'Auld Alliance' with France, and crossed into England with up to 60,000 men on 24 August. But Henry had anticipated this move and had left a substantial army in the north of England under the command of Thomas Howard, Earl of Surrey. The armies clashed on 9 September near Flodden in Northumberland. It proved a devastating defeat for Scotland. Among the 10,000 Scots killed at the Battle of Flodden were 9 earls, 13 barons and King James himself.

SHIFTING ALLIANCES

The Holy League failed to make further progress against France during 1514, and the war petered out. Pope Julius II died that year, and his successor, Leo X, was less interested in military affairs. Ferdinand II left the League, much to the irritation of Henry VIII, who wished to continue the war with France. This marked the moment when Wolsey began to take firmer control of English foreign policy. Until this time, Henry had been inclined to listen to Queen Catherine's advice, which tended to be to listen to her father Ferdinand. Wolsey advised the King to form an alliance with France. A treaty was duly signed in August 1514, and in October Henry offered his sister, Mary Tudor, as a bride to the recently widowed Louis XII. Mary was 18 and known as one of the most beautiful princesses in Europe. The 52-year-old Louis was only too pleased to accept the match. Queen Catherine worried that the alliance with France would threaten her interests, and Spain's, but she could do nothing to stem the growing influence of Wolsey.

It didn't help that there were problems in her marriage to Henry. Soon after their wedding, Catherine had fallen pregnant, but the child, a girl, was stillborn. Four months later, she was pregnant again. She gave birth to a boy, Henry, on New Year's Day 1511 to widespread rejoicing. Sadly, the prince died seven weeks later. Catherine miscarried once again in 1514, and Henry began to wonder if she would ever provide him with a son and heir. As relations grew more strained with Catherine's father, he started seriously contemplating divorce.

Everything changed again in early 1515 with the death of Louis XII, less than three months after his marriage to Mary – according to rumour, he was worn out from his exertions in the bedchamber. He was succeeded by Francis I, who was as charismatic as Henry and even more youthful; a rivalry quickly developed between the two monarchs. When the French conquered Milan at the Battle of Marignano (1515), Wolsey began to favour another alliance with Maximilian and Ferdinand – so Henry and his father-in-law became friends once more.

The sudden death of Ferdinand in January 1516 was a blow to Wolsey's plans. Ferdinand was succeeded by his grandson and Catherine's nephew, Charles V, who immediately pursued peace with France. A month later, Catherine gave birth to a healthy girl, the future Queen Mary I. Henry was encouraged that he might yet gain a male heir, and this period saw a revival in their marriage.

POWER BROKER

Meanwhile, Wolsey continued to seek ways to strengthen English influence in Europe. An opportunity arose in 1517 when Pope Leo X sought to bring an end to the warfare between the European states so that they could concentrate their energies on the external threat from the Ottoman Empire, which was at that time encroaching into the Balkans. In 1518, Wolsey was appointed papal legate and charged with the task of creating this grand peace. In October of that year, the Treaty of London was signed, committing Europe's 20 leading states to peaceful relations. It was seen as a triumph of diplomacy for Wolsey and Henry VIII, placing England at the centre of a new European alliance.

In 1519, Maximilian I, the Holy Roman Emperor, died. Wolsey secretly proposed Henry VIII as a candidate for the post, while publicly supporting King Francis I. In the event, the German princes responsible for electing the new 'King of the Romans' chose Charles V, placing him in control of a substantial swathe of Europe. Francis I was furious. He had spent enormous sums bribing the electors to vote for him. As tensions mounted between Francis and Charles, Wolsey once again spied an opportunity. He put himself forward as mediator, arranging meetings between Henry and the two monarchs in 1520. Francis and Charles were looking to England not so much for mediation as for support, to give them the edge against their rival in a war both of them most likely saw as inevitable. Thus England, for a short time, held the balance of power in Europe.

Henry's meeting with Francis was a spectacular affair known as 'the Field of the Cloth of Gold', where the two Renaissance princes tried to outdo each other in terms of glamour and extravagance. They met on neutral ground, between the English territory of Calais and the kingdom of France. Vast pavilions of cloth encrusted with golden thread and jewels were constructed. Even the ground was spread with embroidered carpets, making it quite literally a field of golden cloth. Witnesses described the temporary city as the eighth wonder of the world. On 7 June 1520, the two kings met and embraced, signalling the start of an 18-day extravaganza of banquets, concerts, jousts and other entertainments. The kings jousted and tilted together. They even wrestled and danced. There was an awkward moment during a wrestling match when Francis threw Henry to the ground, but Henry recovered his dignity by defeating the French king at archery. The Field of the Cloth of Gold achieved little in terms of diplomacy (the two kings would be at war just two years later) but was ruinously expensive – and Henry was fast running out of money.

The Field of the Cloth of Gold, an extravaganza that achieved little and cost much.

DECLINING INFLUENCE

Wolsey's efforts at brokering peace failed, and in 1521 war broke out between Charles and Francis. At a conference in Calais that year, Wolsey tried to bring the sides together, but at the same time (perhaps because he could see which way the wind was blowing) he made a secret treaty with Charles, stating that if Francis would not sign a peace treaty, then England would join the fight against France. Francis continued to pursue war, and in July 1522 England attacked Brittany and Picardy from Calais. The French, already struggling against

Spanish and imperial forces in Italy, could offer little resistance. The war ended in 1525 with a disastrous defeat for France at the Battle of Pavia, in which Francis was captured and many of his chief nobles were killed.

Charles was now supreme in Europe, and no longer had any need of English support. This marked an end to any serious influence for Henry and Wolsey over European affairs. Henry did not, at first, see the writing on the wall. He wished to take advantage of France's weakness and seize the French crown. But Parliament refused to raise taxes for an invasion, so Wolsey introduced the 'Amicable Grant' – effectively a tax without parliamentary approval. The people reacted angrily to the tax, and rebellions broke out across the country from Warwickshire to Kent; these were crushed, but the point had been made and the Amicable Grant was withdrawn. This was the first time that Wolsey had failed to enact the King's will, and the incident may have contributed to his downfall four years later. Henry now realized that his ambitions exceeded his financial means. He was forced to abandon his European dreams and instead made peace with France. No English army would venture abroad again until the Scottish campaign of 1542.

CHAPTER SEVEN

Domestic Affairs

During his 14 years as Lord Chancellor, Thomas Wolsey exercised even greater influence on the home front than in the foreign arena. This was because the king he served was far more interested in the glory that accrued from war and diplomacy than in administering his realm, and Wolsey was given more or less a free hand to manage domestic affairs as he saw fit. He liked to present himself as a man meekly carrying out the wishes of the King. However, his policies often seemed designed to enhance his own wealth, status and power. That is not to say he was entirely self-aggrandizing: it may have been his position as a man of the Church, or his memory of his own humble origins, but many of his reforms seemed genuinely aimed at improving the lot of the poor.

TAXATION

Henry's foreign adventures and extravagant lifestyle required a steady flow of revenue into the royal treasury.

Wolsey, with the assistance of the Treasurer of the Chamber, Sir John Heron, devised a new tax called the subsidy, which sought to tax people based on valuations of their wealth, with one shilling taken from each pound the taxpayer earned. This tax, the basis of today's income tax, was seen as much fairer to poorer members of society than previous fixed-rate forms of taxation. It was successful too, bringing in over £300,000 per year. Wolsey also raised considerable amounts of revenue through 'benevolences' – enforced donations from the nobility. In 1522, when he was trying to finance the war with France, benevolences brought in around £200,000.

At first, Parliament was willing to go along with Wolsey's demands for new taxes. However, in 1515, a legal case involving one Richard Hunne damaged Wolsey's standing, and thereafter Parliament became much less compliant. Hunne was a London-based merchant tailor who fell into a dispute with his priest over non-payment of a mortuary fee following the death of his child. For this he was arrested and imprisoned for heresy. Soon afterwards he was found hanged in his cell, and clergymen were suspected of murdering him. The Bishop of London's chancellor, William Horsey, was accused of complicity in the crime. Although he was released for lack of evidence, the case aroused popular anti-clerical feeling. Eventually, Wolsey felt obliged to come before Parliament and apologize to them on bended knee on behalf of the clergy. He tried to persuade them that as this was a Church matter, Horsey should be tried in Rome, but King Henry rejected the proposal and said it was a matter for the sovereign of the realm. The affair showed up the limits of Wolsey's power and may have emboldened Parliament to stand up to him in future confrontations.

Wolsey's taxes, the subsidy and the benevolences, also soured his relations with the nobility. He was already unpopular with the earls and barons, who resented the power wielded by this upstart butcher's son, and they especially hated the Act of Resumption (1515), which forced many of them to return lands that the King had previously given them as a gift. This build-up of hostility was one of the reasons why Wolsey's attempt to impose the Amicable Grant in 1525 (see page 51) was met with such violent rejection.

LAW

Wolsey's legal reforms were aimed at establishing a justice system that was fair and available to all, including the poor. They also had the effect of concentrating legal power in Wolsey's own hands as the ultimate arbiter of justice.

In the later Middle Ages, most justice was dispensed in common-law courts, which were slow and cumbersome and subject to manipulation by the local nobility. Henry VII started the process of reforming this system with his establishment of the Star Chamber. Wolsey took things further by expanding the scope of the Star Chamber so that plaintiffs could appeal to it in the first instance, not only after they had failed to find remedy in the common-law courts. His aim was to increase people's reliance on the Crown, rather than local lords, to settle their disputes.

He also expanded the Court of Chancery. This was an equity court (making judgements based on conscience, or natural law, rather than common law). Under Wolsey, the number of cases heard by the Court of Chancery grew from about 12 per year in 1509 to over 120 by the mid-1520s. Furthermore, in his desire to deliver justice to the poor, Wolsey established a new court, the Court of Requests, where no fees were required.

As if to prove that no one was above the law, many powerful nobles were convicted and sent to prison by the new courts, including the Earl of Northumberland and Lord Abergavenny. But Wolsey's legal reforms were a victim of their own success, as the courts quickly became overloaded with long and convoluted cases. Wolsey ultimately gave up on his dream of delivering justice for everyone, and in 1528 all but major cases were banned from the Star Chamber.

ENCLOSURES

Wolsey also used his courts to try to tackle the problem of enclosures. Landowners had taken to enclosing areas of common land as well as converting land from arable farming to pastoral farming, which required fewer workers and was therefore more profitable. This led to rural unemployment, mass migration to towns and cities, vagrancy and food shortages, which in turn led to price rises. Wolsey conducted several national enquiries into the issue, and used the Court of Chancery to prosecute 264 landowners for enclosing land, including peers, bishops, knights and Oxford colleges. Yet despite these efforts, the Lord Chancellor could do nothing to stop the enclosures and, as with many of his attempts at reform, he dropped the policy when it became politically expedient to do so: in 1523, Wolsey abandoned his campaign against enclosures in exchange for Parliament's approval of new taxes for Henry's war with France.

THE CHURCH

Thomas Wolsey was in many ways a complex and contradictory figure, and nowhere was this more apparent than in his role as leader of the English Church. He appeared at times to be highly principled, and at other times to be deeply corrupt and power-hungry.

On the positive side, Wolsey took his religious role very seriously, and was prepared to defend the Church at considerable political risk to himself. For example, during the Hunne Affair of 1515, when Parliament was swept up in the general anti-clerical mood, Wolsey refused to permit the passing of a law to diminish the 'benefit of the clergy' (the right of clergymen to be tried in ecclesiastical rather than secular courts).

As papal legate, Wolsey made efforts to improve the reputation of the Church, taking steps to raise the educational level of priests, and in 1519 he encouraged monasteries to embark on a programme of reform. In 1524 and 1527, he closed down 30 corrupt monasteries, and in 1528 he began to impose limits on the benefit of the clergy (due to abuses of the system). That same year he even stood up to Henry, disapproving of the King's choice of a 'woman of dubious virtue' for the position of Abbess of Wilton.

Yet Wolsey failed to carry through many of the reforms he initiated. He could have promoted people to instigate them, yet he didn't. Why? Because he feared losing personal control. He ruled the Church in England like a despot, and in the end his desire to concentrate power in his own hands prevented him from being an effective reformer.

It also led to accusations of hypocrisy. For while Wolsey condemned the corruption of many clergymen, he himself was guilty of pluralism (he held numerous church offices), absenteeism (he was appointed Archbishop of York in 1514, yet didn't visit the city until 1529), simony (the bishops and abbots he appointed had to pay him before they could take up their posts) and ostentatious display of wealth. Despite strictures against sexual relations for clergymen, nepotism and the ordination of minors, Wolsey ordained his own illegitimate teenage son, Thomas Wynter.

Wolsey's corrupt lifestyle and his failure to carry through reforms weakened the Roman Catholic Church in England and ultimately made it easier for Protestantism to take root.

LEGACY

One of the main criticisms of Thomas Wolsey is that, considering all the power he wielded, he actually achieved very little. This may have been because he expended most of his energy in maintaining his own power and reducing the influence of others over the King. He was especially suspicious of the so-called 'minions' (the King's favourites at court) and attempted on many occasions to remove them from the royal presence by giving them jobs in Europe.

His reforms were of secondary importance, and were often dropped if they conflicted with, or no longer served, his political interests. Also, his unwillingness to delegate left him responsible for much of the day-to-day running of the country, and even a man of his administrative talents eventually became overwhelmed. For this reason, he was unable to see through many of the reforms that he initiated.

PART III: HENRY VIII: LATE REIGN: 1527–47

CHAPTER EIGHT

The King's Great Matter

The issue that came to dominate the central years of Henry VIII's reign, and would result in the King's most important legacy to English history, began with a woman. Her name was Anne Boleyn, and in 1525 Henry fell in love with her. Anne was a young lady of the court, and Henry wished to make her his mistress. She would not have been the first. He had indulged in several romantic affairs during the course of his marriage to Catherine, including with Anne's sister Mary. If Anne had yielded to Henry's advances, everything might have turned out differently – but Anne resisted. She wrote to Henry: 'I beseech your highness most earnestly to desist, and to this my answer in good part. I would rather lose my life than my honesty.' Her refusal made Henry even more besotted with her and he continued relentlessly to pursue her. Eventually, Anne told him that she would only yield if he made her his queen.

THE DESIRE FOR A MALE HEIR

Such an idea – that Henry should divorce Catherine and marry Anne – would have been unthinkable were it not for the fact that by the mid-1520s, Henry had grown very unhappy in his marriage. Catherine had by this time borne him several children, but only one of them – Princess Mary – had survived infancy. Henry wanted a male heir to be sure of a stable succession when he died. It was very much the view at this time that a woman would not be strong enough to rule. England's only previous queen, Empress Matilda, had reigned briefly in 1141 during a period of civil war. A more recent civil war, the Wars of the Roses, was within living memory, and Henry may have feared a power struggle after his death if he couldn't produce a son. In 1525, Catherine was 40 and no longer able to bear children.

Henry began to believe that his marriage was cursed and he looked to the Bible for confirmation of this idea. He found it in the Book of Leviticus 20:21: 'And if a man shall take his brother's wife, it is an unclean thing … they shall be childless.' Henry became convinced that Catherine's inability to provide him with a male heir was due to her having been previously married to his brother, Arthur. He also believed that the papal dispensation he had received to allow him to marry Catherine was illegitimate because it was based on the presumption that Catherine was still a virgin when her first husband died. Henry was sure this was not the case, and therefore that the marriage was invalid. For her part, Catherine swore to her dying day that she had been a virgin when she married Henry.

For the next six years, Henry would doggedly pursue what he referred to as his 'Great Matter' – the annulment

Henry VIII's love for Anne Boleyn and the need for a male heir led him to seek the annulment of his marriage with Catherine.

of his marriage. He would devote more energy and research into this project than he did to anything else in his long reign. It would make and destroy several great careers, and ultimately reshape the country.

APPEALS TO THE POPE

The process began on 17 May 1527, when Henry appeared before Cardinal Wolsey in his ecclesiastical court to explain why he had been 'living in sin' with Catherine for so many years. Dutifully, Wolsey took the matter to the Pope, requesting that the marriage be annulled. He argued that, firstly, the original papal dispensation was void because the marriage was against Biblical law; and secondly, the dispensation was incorrectly worded (although a correctly worded version was later found in Spain). He asked the Pope to allow the final decision to be made in England with Wolsey himself (as papal legate) presiding.

Wolsey's appeal placed Pope Clement VII in a difficult position. He was effectively being asked to declare that an earlier Pope had made a mistake in granting the dispensation. Such a declaration risked damaging the Church's moral authority. Moreover, Clement was at that time a virtual prisoner of Charles V, Catherine's nephew. (The Holy Roman Emperor had taken control of Rome in May 1527, during his war with France, Milan, Venice and the Papal States.) Charles was very much against the annulment of his aunt's marriage. Clement was therefore faced with a choice of angering Charles or angering Henry, and he delayed his decision for as long as possible.

Impatient at the delay, Henry decided on a direct appeal to the Pope, bypassing Wolsey. In September 1527, he sent his secretary William Knight to Rome. Because the Pope was under Charles's control, Knight had difficulty gaining access to him, and was not able to deliver his message until December. Knight returned in February, having failed in his mission, so Henry was forced to place the matter once again in the hands of Wolsey.

THE COURT CASE

By April 1528, the Pope had reluctantly granted Henry the right to have the case assessed in England. Two papal legates would preside: Wolsey and Cardinal Campeggio. But Campeggio's journey to England kept being delayed. When he finally arrived in October, it was found that his powers were 'not complete', necessitating further time-consuming negotiations with the papacy. In fact, the Pope had ordered Campeggio to stall the proceedings for as long as possible, and they did not actually get under way until 31 May 1529.

In the courtroom, Catherine kneeled before her husband and made an impassioned speech:

Alas! Sir, wherein have I offended you, or what occasion of displeasure have I deserved? ... This 20 years or more I have been your true wife and by me ye have had divers children, although it hath pleased God to call them out of this world, which hath been no default in me … When ye had me at first, I take God to my judge, I was a true maid, without touch of man. And whether it be true or no, I put it to your conscience. If there be any just cause by the law that ye can allege against me either of dishonesty or any other impediment to banish and put me from you, I am well content to depart to my great shame and dishonour.

In the course of this speech, Henry tried on two occasions to raise Catherine to her feet but she would not be budged. This was her one chance to fight for her marriage in public and she was determined to make the most of it. Catherine won the sympathies of many that day. The Pope approved her appeal for the case to be heard in Rome, and forbade Henry to marry again before a decision was reached. In July 1529, Campeggio adjourned the court. It would never sit again.

THE FALL OF WOLSEY

Wolsey had failed in his mission to give Henry his annulment, and would bear the brunt of the King's anger. Anne Boleyn persuaded the King that Wolsey was treacherous and had deliberately delayed proceedings. Henry probably did not need much convincing. Wolsey's fall was sudden and dramatic. In September he was dismissed from his office as Lord Chancellor and stripped of his properties. Henry himself took over the magnificent York Place, making it his main London residence. By the end of October, Wolsey had been divested of most of his Church titles, but was allowed to remain as Archbishop of York. He travelled to York in April 1530 for the first time in his career.

Wolsey begged Anne to intercede on his behalf, but she refused. He then embarked on a desperate plot to have Anne forced into exile. But his secret communications with Catherine and the Pope were intercepted, and Henry ordered his arrest. Wolsey was accused of treason and ordered to London. In despair, he set out for the capital, remarking: 'If I had served my God as diligently as I did my king, He would not have given me over in my grey hairs.' Wolsey fell ill on the way, and died at Leicester on 29 November 1530. He was 57.

CHAPTER NINE

The Break with Rome

Henry's failure to persuade the Pope to annul his marriage, far from deterring him, only made him more determined to get his way. Over the following years he would embark on a new course of action that would place him on a collision course with the Roman Catholic Church and ultimately bring about a religious reformation in England.

The irony was that throughout his life, Henry was and would remain a devout Catholic. He had no desire to be a part of the Protestant Reformation that was sweeping through northern Europe. Indeed, in 1521, Henry had published a book, *Assertio Septem Sacramentorum* (*Defence of the Seven Sacraments*), affirming the supremacy of the Pope, for which Pope Leo X had awarded him the title Defender of the Faith. Henry was without doubt a firm supporter of the Roman Church. However, his ego was such that he could not let the Pope or anyone else come between him and the fulfilment of his desires.

In October 1529, Henry appointed Sir Thomas More to replace Wolsey as Lord Chancellor. More was a scholar of great renown who had become a personal advisor and friend to Henry. Although he was a staunch Catholic, More proved very willing at first to co-operate with Henry in pursuing the annulment. He denounced Wolsey in Parliament and publicly agreed that the marriage of Henry and Catherine was unlawful. It was only later, when Henry started to deny papal authority, that More's doubts began to grow.

THE RISE OF THOMAS CROMWELL

By then, however, Henry had found a far more effective and ruthless ally in his growing war with Rome: Thomas Cromwell. A former protégé of Cardinal Wolsey, Cromwell rose to favour in late 1530 when the King appointed him to his Privy Council.

Cromwell was a Protestant, who saw Henry's desire for an annulment as the key to ending papal authority in England. He persuaded the King that the only way he would be able to end the marriage with Catherine would be to break with Rome and make himself supreme governor of a new, independent Church of England. That way he could bring about the annulment on his own authority. The policy must have appealed to Henry's pride, for if he did as Cromwell advised, he would no longer owe allegiance to a foreign entity, nor have to submit to the will of a major rival like Charles V. He would be supreme in his own country. Also, it would not have escaped his notice that the Church had enormous landholdings in England and Wales, which would fall into his hands if he became governor of the English Church, vastly inflating his wealth.

Henry began to assert his supremacy over the Church in 1531 by reviving the Statute of Praemunire. This law, first enacted in 1392, forbade obedience to the authority of the Pope or any other foreign ruler. He charged the entire English clergy with praemunire and then demanded £100,000 for their pardon. He further demanded that the clergy recognize him as the 'sole protector and Supreme Head of the Church and clergy of England'. After initial protests, the clergy agreed to his demands. Payment was made in March 1531.

That year also saw changes in the King's private arrangements: in July, Henry officially separated from Catherine and began living openly with Anne Boleyn.

SUPPORT IN PARLIAMENT

By the autumn of 1531, Cromwell was supervising the King's legal and parliamentary affairs. He began manipulating elections to Parliament to ensure that members sympathetic to the annulment were elected. This did not prove too difficult as there was already a strong anticlerical element among Members of Parliament, many of whom begrudged having to pay taxes to Rome to support the papacy. Many had also been influenced by

Thomas Cromwell was the most significant figure of the English Reformation.

the ideas of Protestants such as Germany's Martin Luther, adding a religious element to their desire for an end to papal authority. The Church's separate court system was yet another cause of resentment, especially when canon-law jurists contradicted common-law jurists in their legal judgements.

For all these reasons, there was a groundswell of support for Henry among MPs when Parliament was called into session in January 1532. In March, Parliament passed a petition, drafted by Cromwell, called the 'Supplication Against the Ordinaries', denouncing clerical abuses and the power of the ecclesiastical courts. Henry was described as 'the only head, sovereign lord, protector and defender' of the Church. In May, Henry demanded that the clergy renounce all authority to make laws. This was too much for the Lord Chancellor, Sir Thomas More. He had already refused to acknowledge the King as having jurisdiction over the Church and now begged Henry to relieve him of his office. Henry gave his consent, and on 16 May 1532, More resigned.

In January 1533, Anne Boleyn fell pregnant, adding a degree of urgency to the process. Henry and Anne were secretly married on 25 January, so that the child would be legitimate. This was made easier by the death of the Archbishop of Canterbury, William Warham, a long-time opponent of the annulment. He was replaced by Thomas Cranmer, a fairly minor cleric with Protestant sympathies, who had proved himself a very loyal aide to Henry in the pursuit of his 'Great Matter'.

FORMALIZING THE BREACH

Meanwhile, Cromwell continued to introduce bills to give legislative legitimacy to the growing breach with Rome. In March 1533, the Act of Appeals was passed, suspending all appeals to Rome and effectively ending England's legal ties to the papacy. In April, the Statute in Restraint of Appeals removed the right of the English clergy to appeal to Rome on matters of matrimony, tithes and oblations. This ensured that any decision regarding the King's marriage could not be challenged by the Pope, clearing the way for the King finally to be granted his annulment. On 10 May a formal trial began in Dunstable, and on 23 May – six years and six days after Henry's first appearance in Wolsey's court – Archbishop Cranmer declared Henry's marriage to Catherine to be void. Five days later, he pronounced the King's marriage to Anne to be lawful. Catherine lost her title and Anne was named Queen of England. A furious Pope responded by excommunicating both Henry and Cranmer from the Roman Catholic Church. In September 1533, Anne gave birth to a girl, Elizabeth, who replaced Mary as the legitimate heir to the throne.

In early 1534 a new Parliament was summoned, again under Cromwell's supervision, to enact the legislation necessary to formalize the succession and complete the break with Rome. Parliament duly passed the following new laws:

- **The Act of Succession** named the children of Henry and Anne as heirs to the throne and declared Mary illegitimate. She was now to be styled the Lady Mary rather than Princess Mary.
- **The Act of Dispensations** outlawed the payment of annual tributes by laymen to the Pope, and the **Act**

Concerning Ecclesiastical Appointments and Absolute Restraint of Annates abolished payments by clergymen to the Pope. Through these two acts, the King was able to cut off all revenue flows from England to Rome and divert them to the royal treasury instead. The latter act also handed full control of clerical appointments to the King.

- **The Act of Supremacy** declared that the King was the Supreme Head of the Church of England.
- **The Treasons Act** made it high treason punishable by death to deny royal supremacy over the English Church.
- **The Succession to the Crown Act** required all those asked to take the oath to recognize Anne Boleyn as Henry's lawful wife and their children as legitimate heirs to the throne. Anyone refusing to take the oath was guilty of treason. Sir Thomas More refused to take the oath, and was beheaded on 6 July 1535.

By declaring Henry the Supreme Head of the Church *of* England rather than Head of the Church 'in' England, the schism with the Roman Catholic Church was completed and the English Church was now an entirely distinct and separate institution. This was a truly revolutionary step at the time, as the Catholic Church had reigned for centuries in England and throughout Europe as the ultimate spiritual authority.

The English Reformation, brought about by the Act

of Supremacy and the break with Rome, was gradual in its effects. Some feast days were abolished, pilgrimages were discouraged, and in 1537 a new English Bible was published, but, in many parts of the country, religious life would go on more or less unchanged for years to come. This was not the case for one sector of society, however. For England's Catholic monasteries, an era of turmoil and destruction was about to ensue.

CHAPTER TEN

The Dissolution of the Monasteries

Monasteries had been a feature of the English landscape since before there was an England. Monasticism had played a key role in English Christianity from the very beginning. In fact, the Anglo-Saxons were converted to Christianity by monastic missionaries. The Cistercian order in particular had been influential in England since the twelfth century.

A DECLINING INSTITUTION

By the time of Henry VIII, however, monasticism was in decline. The Black Death of the fourteenth century had severely reduced the number of monks, and during the early Tudor period monasteries were regularly accused of scandalous misbehaviour. Protestant tracts charged nuns with the murder of infants resulting from their promiscuous lives. Cardinal Wolsey was forced to close down a number of monastic houses for corrupt practices, with the blessing of the Pope.

In truth, most monasteries at this time were not especially corrupt, although not especially religious either. Only three small orders, the Bridgettines, Franciscan Observants and Carthusians, were noted for strict piety. The vast majority of monks and nuns lived comfortable, quiet and happy lives in their communities.

What were the monasteries?

In 1509, there were more than 850 religious houses in England and Wales. Although collectively termed monasteries, they were individually referred to by different names, depending on their size. The largest were called abbeys, medium-sized ones were usually known as priories or nunneries, and the smallest were called friaries.

Some monasteries were 'closed' – meaning the monks lived within their walls and did not interact with outsiders. Others were 'open' – their occupants worked with the local community, helping the sick and teaching local boys. Usually, open monasteries were poor, as any money they made was spent on charitable works, while closed monasteries could be very wealthy.

Collectively, the closed houses owned about one-third of all the land in England and Wales. The 30 richest monasteries were as rich as, or richer than, the wealthiest nobles in the country. Much of the land they owned had been bequeathed to them in people's wills.

WHY DID HENRY SET HIS SIGHTS ON THE MONASTERIES?
The monasteries represented the last great bastion of papal authority in England and Wales, and Henry may have feared that, even after he had declared himself head of the Church, they would remain secretly loyal to the Pope. But mixed in with this political incentive for attacking the monasteries, there must have been a financial one as well.

By the mid-1530s, Henry was short of money and was disinclined to risk unpopularity by demanding a new tax from Parliament. It could not have escaped his notice that many of the monasteries were extremely wealthy, and seizing their assets would certainly help replenish the royal coffers.

To stir up popular anger against the monasteries, Cromwell let it be known that a large portion of their annual income went to the Vatican. However, the government knew very well that little monastic income went abroad – their wealth remained in England and was therefore highly accessible.

INVESTIGATING THE MONASTERIES
In January 1535, Henry appointed Cromwell to the offices of Royal Vicegerent and Vicar-General, responsible for the day-to-day running of the Church. He ordered him to visit all religious houses in the country to check on their standards of morality. The aim of this exercise was to give Henry political and religious justification for his planned attack. Cromwell delegated the

task to men loyal to him, including Richard Layton, Thomas Legh, John ap Rice and John Tregonwell. These were ambitious men, keen to impress Cromwell, and they knew what was expected of them. They deliberately went in search of evidence of moral laxity, including sexual promiscuity and the superstitious worship of relics.

In their interviews at each house, they actively encouraged members and servants to confess to immoral behaviour as well as inform on one another. If no evidence of sin was uncovered, nothing was reported. When compared to other contemporary accounts, their reports appear exaggerated and distorted, often recalling scandals from years before and putting the worst possible interpretation on what they heard. Some houses protested that Layton and Legh used bullying tactics, but Cromwell ignored such complaints.

At the same time, the King commissioned the *Valor Ecclesiasticus*, a detailed survey of the finances of the Church in England, Wales and the English-controlled parts of Ireland, in order to assess how much tax the Church should pay. Local commissioners were sent out in each area to interview clergymen, heads of monasteries and other churchmen to find out the details of their income and property.

DISSOLUTION OF THE SMALLER MONASTERIES

The King needed to establish a legal basis for the disbanding of the monasteries, and also ensure that their wealth would come to him after he closed them down, rather than be inherited by the descendents of the institutions' founders. So, in March 1536, Parliament enacted the Suppression of Religious Houses Act. This stated that any religious house with an annual income of less than £200 (as assessed by the *Valor Ecclesiasticus*) was to be dissolved and its assets would revert to the King. The act was ostensibly prompted by the reports already coming in from Cromwell's agents. Its preamble read, in part:

> *FORASMUCH as manifest sin, vicious, carnal and abominable living is daily used and committed among the little and small abbeys, priories and other religious houses of monks, canons and nuns, where the congregation of such religious persons is under the number of twelve persons, whereby the governors of such religious houses, and their convent, spoil, destroy, consume and utterly waste ... Such small houses [will] be utterly suppressed, and the religious persons therein committed to great and honourable monasteries of religion in this realm, where they may be compelled to live religiously, for reformation of their lives, there can else be no redress nor reformation in that behalf.*

The reason for the decision to target the smaller houses first is not clear, as these were not necessarily more immoral than the larger houses, according to the reports from Cromwell's men. It may have been a pragmatic decision, because the smaller houses were less likely to offer much opposition.

About 330 religious houses fell into the category defined by the act. Some 80 of these were spared by the King because their sins were deemed not too serious (or because they had contacts in the government who could use their influence to save them), but they did have to pay a large fine – usually a year's income – in return for their reprieve. The fines earned the King around £13,500 in total.

The rest were closed down during 1536, their assets appropriated by the King's agents. The agents acted with speed, in case monasteries tried to move their wealth and treasure to a safe place before they could be seized. Any gold, silver, bronze or lead was melted down. All other removable items were auctioned off to locals, and the land was rented out. The fabric of the buildings – bricks, panelling, doors and the like – was purloined by grateful locals, and many monasteries quickly became ruins.

As for the inhabitants of the monasteries, the heads of the houses were offered a pension, while the other residents were given the choice of transferring to a larger monastery or going to live in society. If they chose the latter, they were allowed to renounce any vows of poverty and obedience, but not chastity.

PILGRIMAGE OF GRACE
The dissolution of the smaller monasteries proceeded smoothly in some parts of the country, such as the

south-west, and less so in others. It met with particular opposition in the north, where it sparked one of the most serious of all the rebellions of the Tudor period, the Pilgrimage of Grace. This was a popular protest against Henry's break with Rome, the casting off of Catherine of Aragon and her replacement with Anne Boleyn, and the Dissolution of the Monasteries. Most of the anger was directed not at the King himself but at his chief minister, Thomas Cromwell.

A prelude to the rebellion, known as the Lincolnshire Rising, broke out on 2 October 1536 and culminated on 14 October when some 40,000 people – mostly commoners but also some nobles – marched on Lincoln and occupied the cathedral, demanding protection for Lincolnshire's religious houses. The King ordered them to disperse or face the forces of Charles Brandon, Duke of Suffolk. Most of the protesters departed, and the leaders of the demonstration were soon rounded up and executed.

The Lincolnshire Rising inspired the Pilgrimage of Grace, which began on 13 October. It was led by Robert Aske, a barrister from an eminent Yorkshire family. Aske and his 9,000 followers marched into York and occupied the city. They then entered the city's monasteries and expelled the newly installed tenants, arranging for the monks and nuns to return to their houses. Aske was an able organizer and a fine orator; it was he who coined the phrase 'Pilgrimage of Grace', deliberately defining the protest in religious terms. His followers were well disciplined and attracted support from many parts of Yorkshire. By 21 October they numbered 35,000. The King had no choice but to negotiate with them. Thomas Howard, Duke of Norfolk, representing the King, met with Aske and his supporters. Norfolk promised a general pardon and a Parliament to be held at York within a year; the monasteries could be reprieved until Parliament had met. Aske trusted the promises and dismissed his followers.

In February 1537, a new uprising took place in Cumberland and Westmorland under Sir Francis Bigod. The rebellion was not authorized by Aske, but after it was put down, Henry used it as an excuse to arrest not only Bigod but Aske and the other organizers of the original Pilgrimage of Grace. They were all executed.

DISSOLUTION OF THE LARGER MONASTERIES

Early in 1538, Cromwell began to move against the friaries (exempted in the previous round because they were so poor) and the larger religious houses. Once again, he sent out his commissioners, including Layton and Legh. Most of the friaries, abbeys and monasteries surrendered voluntarily, having witnessed the forced closures of 1536 and the violent suppression of the Pilgrimage of Grace. Those heads of houses who co-operated were given pensions for life and other privileges. Those who offered resistance were forcefully turned out and given no pensions. In 1539, Parliament passed the

Act for the Dissolution of the Greater Monasteries, which gave legal backing to the process. Some still resisted, including the abbots of Colchester, Glastonbury and Reading, who were hanged, drawn and quartered for treason. The last monastery to be closed was Waltham Abbey in April 1540.

EFFECTS OF THE DISSOLUTION

In all, more than 800 religious houses were closed in the dissolutions, home to in excess of 10,000 monks, nuns, friars and canons. Most monks and nuns were treated well and given reasonably generous pensions. Many became clergymen. The servants who worked at the monasteries fared far worse as they did not receive a pension.

The dissolution led to the transfer of vast tracts of land to the Crown. The King also acquired huge amounts of gold and silver, worth up to a million pounds. All this might have made the Crown financially independent for generations, with no further need to call Parliament – had Henry exploited it prudently. However, his need for cash, especially to fight wars against France and Scotland between 1543 and 1547, led him to sell off the land at bargain prices. Thus it was not the King who ultimately benefited from the dissolution but the gentry who bought the lands. This new class increased in power and independence, and now had a vested interest in ensuring that the Reformation was maintained and Roman Catholicism was never fully restored.

Seizing the assets of the monasteries might have made the Crown financially independent had Henry VIII not wasted his new wealth on financing war.

CHAPTER ELEVEN

Court Manoeuvres

While the Dissolution of the Monasteries was proceeding around the country, dramatic changes were taking place at court. In January 1536, Anne Boleyn miscarried for the second time. After three years of marriage she had failed to give Henry his longed-for son. When Henry realized the second miscarried baby had been a boy, he began to believe that his marriage to Anne was cursed.

THE DOWNFALL OF ANNE BOLEYN

Anne's position was already precarious. She had attracted some powerful enemies at court, including the chief minister Thomas Cromwell and the Duke of Suffolk. The Boleyn family were steadily losing influence. For example, they supported an alliance with France rather than the Holy Roman Empire, but Henry, advised by Cromwell, favoured closer ties with the Emperor. Anne also had former supporters of Queen Catherine ranged against her, and they were now pushing for Henry to recognize his daughter Mary, who had reached maturity.

While Anne was recovering from the second miscarriage, Henry took one of her ladies in waiting, Jane Seymour, as his mistress. He declared that he had been seduced into marrying Anne by sortilege (meaning deception or sorcery). In April 1536, five men, including Anne's brother, were arrested on suspicion of having had sexual relations with the Queen. On 2 May, Anne was arrested on charges of adultery and witchcraft. There is a strong likelihood that Cromwell was behind the plot to bring down Anne, although no proof. She was duly convicted, and imprisoned in the Tower of London. The five accused men were also found guilty, and were executed on 17 May. That same day, Archbishop Cranmer declared Henry's marriage to Anne invalid, making her daughter Elizabeth illegitimate. Anne was beheaded on 19 May by a French swordsman – the first English queen to be publicly executed.

Eleven days after Anne's execution, Henry married Jane Seymour. In June, Parliament passed the second Act of Succession, which declared Henry's children by Jane to be next in line of succession. On 12 October 1537, Jane gave birth to a son, Prince Edward. Henry was overjoyed to have a male heir at last – yet Jane's death from an infection 12 days later seemed to affect him deeply. He wore black for three months and did not remarry for three years, during which time he began to put on a lot of weight.

THE FALL OF THOMAS CROMWELL

In his personal beliefs, Henry remained a Catholic, despite having instigated the break with Rome, and he became increasingly concerned about the extent of religious changes being instituted by Thomas Cromwell and Thomas Cranmer. The conservative faction at court, led by Thomas Howard, Duke of Norfolk, saw its opportunity, and succeeded in passing through Parliament the Act of Six Articles (1539), which reaffirmed traditional Catholic doctrine on the Mass, the Sacraments and the priesthood.

Meanwhile, Cromwell was busy trying to find a suitable new bride for the King. He looked to Europe, hoping to make an alliance with a Protestant country to help fend off the threat from the Roman Catholic powers of France and the Holy Roman Empire. For most of the 1530s this had been a minor issue, as Henry and Francis were enjoying a period of good relations, while Charles V was distracted with internal problems within his kingdoms. But when Charles and Francis made peace in January 1539, the possibility of an anti-English, Roman Catholic alliance began to worry Henry.

Cromwell suggested that Henry marry Anne, sister of William, Duke of Cleves (a duchy on the lower Rhine), who could be a useful ally in the event of a Franco-German invasion. The painter Hans Holbein the Younger was sent to Cleves to paint her portrait. The painting may have flattered her – certainly it convinced Henry to agree to wed Anne without having met her. Soon after the wedding in January 1540, however, he sought to annul the marriage. Anne did not object. She was given the title 'The King's Sister', two houses and a generous allowance.

Henry was angry with Cromwell for having coaxed him into this ill-starred match. It had not even proved politically useful, as the feared Franco-Imperial alliance had failed to materialize. This, together with the King's uneasiness with Cromwell's Protestant reforms, meant that Cromwell's days as the King's chief minister were numbered. Meanwhile, Cromwell's enemy the Duke of Norfolk attempted to elevate his own status at court by introducing Henry to his young and attractive niece, Catherine Howard. Henry immediately fell for her. Cromwell, though shrewd enough to realize that he was now politically isolated, could do nothing.

In June 1540, Cromwell was arrested and imprisoned in the Tower. A long list of charges was levelled against him, including the protection of Protestants accused of heresy, failing to enforce the Act of Six Articles, and even plotting to marry the King's daughter, Mary. He was beheaded on Tower Hill on 28 July.

CATHERINE HOWARD AND CATHERINE PARR

On the day of Cromwell's execution, Henry married Catherine Howard. He was besotted with his new queen and showered her with gifts, including lands formerly belonging to Cromwell. The Duke of Norfolk, who had also been uncle to Anne Boleyn and had seen his power at court wane with her execution, now enjoyed a revival of his influence. Henry and Catherine toured England together in the summer of 1541. However, by the autumn, rumours had started to circulate about Catherine's past – namely that she had been engaged to a courtier named Francis Dereham before she became queen. In November, Archbishop Cranmer interrogated her about this. If Catherine had admitted to the engagement, her marriage to Henry would have been declared unlawful. She would have been banished from court, but possibly spared execution. Catherine, however, denied the engagement, claiming that Dereham had raped her. Cranmer then came across rumours of an affair between Catherine and another courtier, Thomas Culpeper, after her marriage to Henry. Both parties denied the allegations, but a letter from Catherine to Culpeper, along with testimony from members of her household, provided Cranmer with the evidence he sought. Catherine was stripped of her title as queen and imprisoned on 23 November. Dereham and Culpeper were executed on 10 December, and Catherine was beheaded on 13 February 1542.

In July 1543, Henry was married for the sixth and final time, to a wealthy widow named Catherine Parr. Catherine, a friend of Mary Tudor, helped reconcile the King to his daughters from previous marriages. She also influenced Henry's decision to pass the Third Succession

Act of 1543, which restored Mary and Elizabeth to the line of succession, behind their half-brother Edward. Catherine had Protestant sympathies and engaged in frequent arguments with Henry about religion. But Henry remained a Catholic at heart, albeit one prepared to tolerate limited reform.

COURT FACTIONS

The King's ambivalence over the question of religious reform helped stir up factionalism at court. There were two main factions: the conservatives, in favour of a return to Catholicism, led by the Duke of Norfolk and Stephen Gardiner, Bishop of Winchester; and the reformers – supporters of Protestant reform – led by Archbishop Cranmer, Charles Brandon (Duke of Suffolk), Catherine Parr and Edward Seymour, Prince Edward's uncle. Both factions competed to wield influence over Henry and – looking ahead – young Edward.

In 1543, the Norfolk-Gardiner faction tried on three occasions to charge Cranmer with heresy. Each time they failed because Henry intervened to save the archbishop. In 1546, Gardiner drew up an arrest warrant for Queen Catherine, again on grounds of heresy, but she was able to persuade Henry of her innocence. Later that year, the tables were turned when Norfolk found himself in trouble, along with his son the Earl of Surrey, accused of plotting to make Norfolk regent for the young Edward upon Henry's death. They were charged with treason and imprisoned in the Tower. Surrey was executed in January 1547. Norfolk evaded the axeman, however, because Henry died before his sentence could be carried out.

WARS WITH SCOTLAND AND FRANCE

Following his break with Rome, Henry feared the possibility of an anti-English Catholic alliance between Scotland and France. This prospect became more likely in 1537 with the marriage between King James V of Scotland and Mary of Guise, daughter of a powerful French noble. In 1542, Henry decided to launch a pre-emptive attack on Scotland. King Francis I of France was preoccupied with a war against the Holy Roman Emperor Charles V, so James could not call upon French support. Henry raised an army in the north, then summoned James to England to sign a treaty of friendship. James refused, and in October the English army invaded. They inflicted a decisive defeat on the Scots at Solway Moss in November. A month later, James was dead, leaving his six-day-old daughter Mary as the new monarch of Scotland.

Many Scottish nobles were captured at Solway Moss. In exchange for their release, they had to agree to the Treaty of Greenwich, which proposed uniting England and Scotland through the marriage of Henry's son Edward and the infant Queen of Scots, Mary. But Henry overplayed his hand with his demand that all Scots swear fealty to the King of England. In 1543, the Scottish

Parliament repealed all its treaties with England and reaffirmed those it had signed with France. Angered by this defiance, Henry launched two more invasions of Scotland, in 1544 and 1545. His armies caused wanton destruction to farms and villages in the borders, and even captured Edinburgh. This marked the beginning of an eight-year conflict known as the Rough Wooing, because England's aim was to force Scotland to agree to the match between Mary and Edward.

In 1544, Henry was increasingly concerned that France was about to come to Scotland's aid, so he made a military alliance with Charles V and declared war on France. But Charles soon reneged on the agreement and negotiated a truce with Francis. This freed up Francis to turn his attention to an invasion of England that would, in his words, 'liberate the English from the Protestant tyranny' that Henry had imposed upon them. In May 1545, the French assembled a huge fleet, even bigger than the Spanish Armada that would threaten England 43 years later. On 18 July, the French force, composed of 150 warships, 25 war galleys and over 30,000 troops, arrived in the Solent, but they were beaten back from Portsmouth Harbour by an English fleet of some 80 ships. The famous English battleship *Mary Rose* sank during this campaign. After staging a brief invasion of the Isle of Wight, the French force retreated.

The wars with Scotland and France cost Henry over £3 million, but achieved virtually nothing. If anything, they strengthened the Auld Alliance between England's two traditional enemies. To help pay for the wars, Henry began to debase the national coinage by mixing base metals with the silver. Soon the coins were almost entirely copper, and Henry became known as 'old coppernose' from the appearance of his profile on the coins. Debasement raised some money, but also led to rapid inflation as people lost faith in the currency and began hoarding their old silver coins. Foreign goods became much more expensive, with merchants on the Continent refusing to accept the new copper coins for their wares.

DEATH AND LEGACY

Henry's health steadily deteriorated during the 1540s. He became morbidly obese, and required the help of mechanical contraptions to move about. A leg wound, possibly from a jousting accident in 1536, began to fester and become ulcerated. He suffered frequent headaches, which may have contributed to his mood swings and unpredictable behaviour. Perhaps through Catherine's influence, he began to entertain Protestant views on the sacraments in 1546. Yet at the same time he entered into secret negotiations with a papal envoy regarding the possibility of submitting England once more to the supremacy of the Pope.

Henry died in his bed at Whitehall Palace on 28 January 1547. He was 55 years old. The formerly handsome and popular young king ended his reign as a grotesquely fat tyrant, feared by many. His reign can, in many ways, be judged a failure. Despite his obsession with producing a legitimate male heir, his son Edward was a sickly boy who would outlive his father by just six years. And despite years of costly warfare, England remained menaced by enemies abroad. Yet Henry could boast some solid achievements, including the incorporation of Wales into his kingdom in 1536, and the creation of a large and powerful navy. His most important legacy, however, was an accidental one: his break with Rome set in train a process which he neither anticipated nor desired, but which would lead, in time, to a fully Protestant England.

PART IV: EDWARD VI (1547–53) AND MARY I (1553–58)

CHAPTER TWELVE

The Lord Protector

Henry VIII was laid to rest at Windsor on 16 February 1547. In accordance with his wishes, his body was placed in the same tomb as his beloved Jane Seymour. Four days later, Jane and Henry's son Edward was crowned at Westminster Abbey. The new king, who was the sixth Edward to rule England, was just nine years old. The coronation ceremony was shortened in case it proved wearisome to the young king, and also because the Reformation had rendered some parts of the service inappropriate. Archbishop Cranmer, presiding over the coronation, affirmed the King's supremacy over the Church of England and urged Edward to continue with the Reformation. Afterwards, Edward presided at a banquet in Westminster Hall, where he dined wearing his crown on his head. Yet despite his headware, everyone knew that Edward was king in name only – and would remain so until he reached adulthood. Real power now resided with his uncle, Edward Seymour, the regent, known as the Lord Protector.

THE REGENT'S NEPHEW

Edward, the only legitimate son of Henry VIII, was born on 12 October 1537. His mother, Jane Seymour, died within days of his birth, and he was placed in the care

Edward VI, the boy king. It was during his brief reign that England officially renounced Catholicism to become a Protestant country.

of Lady Margaret Bryan. Edward's health was never very robust, and his father did everything he could to protect him, calling the prince 'this whole realm's most precious jewel'. He lavished every luxury and comfort on his son, including a troupe of minstrels. He provided Edward with 14 highborn children to be his playmates and fellow students. The prince received a first-class education and showed signs of a sharp intellect. He was also trained in fencing and horseback riding, but was always happier with a book in his hands. Edward developed a close relationship with his stepmother Catherine Parr, who encouraged him to embrace the Protestant faith. Edward also got on well with his half-sister Elizabeth, just four years his senior and similarly receptive to Protestant ideas. Mary, 21 years older and a devout Catholic, was a more distant figure in his life.

EDWARD SEYMOUR

Before he died, Henry VIII made arrangements for how England should be governed during Edward's minority. To avoid having a Protector, who might concentrate power in his own hands, Henry entrusted government to a 'Council of Regency' that would rule collectively, by majority decision. Yet within days of Henry's death, Edward Seymour made his bid for supreme power.

Edward Seymour was born in around 1505, the son of a prominent courtier, Sir John Seymour, and brother of King Henry VIII's third wife, Jane. Her marriage to the king was a great boost to Edward's career. He served as Lord Admiral from 1542 to 1543 and fought in Scotland and France between 1544 and 1546. By the time of Henry's death, he was one of the leading political figures in the land. Seymour was a committed Protestant, and determined to prevent the conservative Catholic faction from taking power on Henry's death and reversing all of Cranmer's religious reforms.

Seymour managed to convince, cajole or bribe a majority of the executors of Henry's will to appoint him Lord Protector of the Realm. He was lucky in his timing as both his major rivals from the conservative faction – the Duke of Norfolk and Stephen Gardiner – had been removed from the centre of power at the time of Henry's death. Seymour, who by now had been created Duke of Somerset, was quick to consolidate his authority. In March, he obtained an official letter from the king allowing him to make appointments to the Privy Council and to call meetings with the council at his own discretion. This allowed him to rule very much like a monarch, with the Privy Council operating as little more than a rubber stamp. The only immediate opposition he faced was from the Chancellor, Thomas Wriothesley, a member of the conservative faction, and also from his own brother, Thomas Seymour. Somerset quickly dismissed Wriothesley from the chancellorship on charges of corruption. His brother proved a more challenging opponent.

THOMAS SEYMOUR

Somerset had tried to win Thomas over with offers of titles and a seat on the Privy Council, but Thomas, jealous of his brother, began plotting to overthrow him. He tried to win over King Edward by smuggling him pocket money. Thomas advised the King that in two years he should rid himself of the Protector and 'rule as other kings do'. King Edward, shrewdly, refused to co-operate. At the same time, Thomas attempted to raise his status and influence by wooing Henry VIII's widow, Catherine Parr. Her household included the 11-year-old Lady Jane Grey, first cousin once removed to the King, and the 13-year-old Elizabeth Tudor. In the spring of 1547, Thomas and Catherine secretly married. The following year, a pregnant Catherine discovered her husband embracing Elizabeth. She immediately removed Elizabeth to the household of a friend. In September 1548, Catherine died in childbirth, and Thomas was soon writing love letters to Elizabeth. She, however, spurned his advances.

Frustrated by his inability to manipulate either Edward or Elizabeth, Thomas's thoughts began to turn towards open rebellion. He tried to foment opposition to Somerset's authority among the nobility. As Lord High Admiral, he spoke with pirates on the western coasts – the very people it was his duty to suppress – hoping to secure their support in an uprising. On the night of 16 January 1549, Thomas broke into the King's apartments at Hampton Court Palace – perhaps planning to kidnap Edward. In the process he awoke one of the King's spaniels and shot it dead. The next day, he was arrested and sent to the Tower of London. Very soon, all his schemes began to come to light. He was accused and convicted of 33 acts of treason. On 20 March 1549, he was beheaded.

WAR, RELIGION AND REBELLION

Somerset, a soldier by background, was intent on pursuing the war with Scotland and forcing the Scots to accept the marriage between Mary, their queen, and King Edward. Following a decisive victory at the Battle of Pinkie Cleugh in September 1547, Somerset established a network of garrisons in Scotland, stretching as far north as Dundee. But the Scots refused to submit. Their French allies sent reinforcements to defend Edinburgh in 1548. Meanwhile Mary, Queen of Scots was moved to France where she was betrothed to the Dauphin, the French crown prince. The cost of maintaining the garrisons began to strain the royal treasury, and when the French attacked Boulogne in August 1549 (the port had been seized by Henry VIII in 1544), Somerset began to withdraw his armies from Scotland. The French cut off supplies to Boulogne, but an English naval victory over the French off the Channel Islands ensured that Boulogne could be supplied, and the English clung on.

At home, Somerset undertook a series of ambitious

religious reforms, turning England into a truly Protestant realm. In 1549 Archbishop Cranmer compiled a Book of Common Prayer, its use in churches enforced by an Act of Uniformity, and this became the standard liturgy for the Anglican Church. Cranmer changed doctrine on the Eucharist, legalized clerical marriage, imposed compulsory services in English, and ended the veneration of saints and the use of images in worship.

The enforcement of church services in English provoked an uprising in 1549 in Devon and Cornwall, sometimes called the Prayer Book Rebellion. The rebellion was easily dealt with but, put together with failures in Scotland and the threat to Boulogne, added to Somerset's growing reputation for mismanagement.

However, the main cause of his downfall was his hostility to land enclosures. Somerset believed in giving peasants security of land tenure, and wished to curtail the practice by rich landowners of enclosing areas hitherto regarded as common land. In 1548 and 1549, he sent out commissions of enquiry to investigate complaints by villagers. This brought him into conflict with Parliament, most of whose members were themselves landowners. Serious opposition to Somerset began to form under the leadership of John Dudley, Earl of Warwick.

Somerset's stance also had the effect of encouraging peasants in Norfolk to rise up against the landlords, believing they were acting with the full support of the Lord Protector. Kett's Rebellion, as it became known, broke out in July 1549, led by a yeoman farmer, Robert Kett. Under his command, a rebel army numbering 16,000 stormed Norwich on 21 July. The rebels were ultimately defeated by an army led by Dudley, Earl of Warwick, on 27 August. Kett was tried for treason and hanged from the walls of Norwich Castle in December 1549.

By the autumn of 1549, Somerset had lost the support of most of his councillors. In October, John Dudley led a coup against him, ousting him from office. Dudley had already prepared the ground for his assumption of power by winning the support of the King and the Privy Council and, by January 1550, was *de facto* regent.

CHAPTER THIRTEEN

The Duke of Northumberland

Dudley decided not to take the title Lord Protector. He preferred to cultivate a more low-key image, perhaps because it made him less of a potential target for opponents. Nevertheless, he was careful to keep the important levers of power within his control. In February he became Lord President of the Council, with the power to appoint and dismiss councillors. A Protestant, like Somerset, he was thus able to remove dangerous conservatives, such as the Earl of Southampton, from influence. By making himself Grand Master of the Household he could control and supervise the Privy Chamber – the people with access to the King. To impress his followers, Dudley raised himself to a dukedom, becoming Duke of Northumberland in October 1551. He tried to reconcile with Somerset and even had his son and heir marry Somerset's daughter. But Somerset continually tried to obstruct and rally opposition to Northumberland's policies. Aware of his precarious position, Northumberland felt he could take no chances: Somerset was convicted of raising an army without a licence, and was executed in January 1552.

John Dudley, the Duke of Northumberland, was one of the most influential people in King Edward VI's court, but he carefully avoided taking the title of Lord Protector.

RULING THE KINGDOM

Northumberland's power was largely based on his close relationship with the King. His aim was to become indispensable in that role, so that when Edward came of age, Northumberland could move seamlessly into the position of principal minister. He hoped for a smooth transition when the time came, and for this to happen he needed Edward to grow into his authority as quickly as possible. So the King was regularly briefed on decisions of the Council, and from the age of 14, Edward's signature on documents no longer needed Council members' countersignatures.

Northumberland was determined to avoid the rebellions that had characterized the period of the Protectorate. He passed a new law 'for the punishment of unlawful assemblies', and granted licenses for the establishment of local cavalry units to keep order in the countryside. At the same time, he attempted to alleviate the suffering of the poor by repealing the harsh 1547 'Act for the Punishment of Vagabonds' and passing a Poor Law, which made provision for weekly parish-based collections for relief of the poor. While upholding landlords' rights to enclose common land, he ensured that any landlords guilty of illegal enclosures were prosecuted. The measures proved effective, and there was no more unrest during his time in office.

The problems of coin debasement, a legacy of Henry VIII's last years, persisted, together with crippling royal debts from recent wars, adding up to a serious financial crisis. Northumberland called in the financial expert Thomas Gresham, who, within a short time, managed to stabilize the value of the currency and start the work of reducing the Crown's debts.

Northumberland pursued religious reform with even more vigour than his predecessor Somerset. A revised version of the Book of Common Prayer, issued in 1552, rejected the idea of transubstantiation. And a new set of doctrinal statements, the Forty-Two Articles, was issued in June 1553. The Articles proclaimed 'justification by faith' (in other words, people could be saved by faith alone) and denied the existence of purgatory.

Embarrassingly for Northumberland, the resolutely Catholic Mary Tudor ignored the reforms and refused to have the Book of Common Prayer in any of her residences. She continued to hear Catholic Mass in her chapel, along with her entire household and a throng of regular visitors. When Northumberland tried to put pressure on her to stop, first she threatened to flee the country, then she sent the ambassador of the Holy Roman Empire to threaten Northumberland with war. In the end a compromise was reached whereby Mary continued to hear Mass but in a more private manner.

The religious reforms were equally unpopular with many in the clergy. Northumberland dismissed a number of troublemaking conservative bishops from their posts, replacing them with reformists, including evangelical

Protestants such as John Hooper and John Ponet. At the same time, he found a way of raising revenue by stripping the bishoprics of substantial landholdings and adding these to the Crown lands.

Northumberland also helped the royal finances by putting an end to expensive foreign wars. In January 1550, he agreed the withdrawal of the besieged English garrison at Boulogne, handing the port back to France for the sum of 400,000 crowns – far less than the two million crowns Henry VIII had originally offered to sell it for, but a welcome cash injection nonetheless. In March, Northumberland concluded the Treaty of Boulogne with France, bringing an end to the conflict. In 1551, he cemented the peace by arranging the betrothal of Edward to the six-year-old Elisabeth of Valois, daughter of the French king, Henry II. He also agreed a peace treaty with Scotland, part of which included the first attempt in history to establish an exact boundary between the two nations – agreed with French arbitration in 1552.

DEATH OF THE KING

In February 1553, Edward fell seriously ill with tuberculosis, and it soon became clear that he was dying. Northumberland knew he had to act fast to prevent Mary Tudor from succeeding. If she became queen, she would restore England to Catholicism, undoing all his reforms, and almost certainly he would lose his head.

Northumberland realized that if they were to disinherit

Mary on grounds of illegitimacy, they would have to do the same to Elizabeth (she, too, being the issue of an 'invalid' marriage), even though she embraced the Church of England. So he began making arrangements to install Lady Jane Grey, the ardently Protestant granddaughter of Henry VIII's younger sister, as the next in line to the throne. On 21 May 1553, Lady Jane was married to Northumberland's son, Guildford Dudley. From this point on, Northumberland's star was firmly hitched to that of Lady Jane – he would rise or fall with her.

Northumberland urged Edward to approve a new order of succession, bypassing his two half-sisters and naming Lady Jane Grey as his successor. Edward did not need much persuading. He wrote a document called 'My devise for the Succession'. In the first draft, when he still believed he might survive his illness, his concern was to provide for a male succession. After declaring Mary and Elizabeth illegitimate, he stated that he wished to be succeeded by the son that he hoped Lady Jane Grey might produce. But around the end of May or early June, Edward's condition greatly deteriorated, and he changed the document to the effect that Lady Jane herself should inherit the crown. Questions were raised in the Council as to the legality of the 'devise', causing Northumberland to lose his temper. To reinforce its legitimacy, the devise was prepared as letters patent and, on 21 June, it was signed by more than a hundred notables, including members of the Privy Council, peers, bishops and judges.

Preparations were made to have it passed in Parliament in September.

As Edward approached death, Mary was summoned to London so that she could visit her brother for the last time. Before she left, she was warned that this was a trap set by Northumberland to capture her. So Mary went instead to her estates in East Anglia, a stronghold of Catholicism.

Edward died on 6 July 1553. He was 15 years of age.

THE NINE-DAY QUEEN

Northumberland delayed announcing the news of the King's death while he gathered his forces. He sent ships to the Norfolk coast to prevent Mary's escape or the arrival of reinforcements from the Continent. Meanwhile, Mary set about raising an army. Large numbers rallied to her cause – not just Catholics, but those who believed that her lawful claim to the throne outweighed any religious considerations.

Mary dispatched a letter to the Privy Council, demanding to be recognized as queen. It arrived on 10 July, the same day Lady Jane Grey was proclaimed queen in the streets of London. The Council replied that Jane was queen by Edward's authority and that Mary was illegitimate. Yet Northumberland could tell that many councillors were nervous and ready to defect. Though a seasoned soldier, he was in two minds about leading an army in pursuit of Mary, as he would then no longer be in control of events in London. But Queen Jane reassured him that her father, the Duke of Suffolk, would look after things in his absence.

So on 14 July, Northumberland departed for East Anglia at the head of 1,500 troops and artillery. As he approached, reports came to him of the growing strength of Mary's forces, now numbering nearly 20,000. Northumberland decided to retreat to Cambridge. Back in London, popular opinion was firmly on the side of Mary, and the Privy Council realized that it had gravely miscalculated. On 19 July, led by the Earl of Arundel and the Earl of Pembroke, the Council publicly proclaimed Mary as queen, sparking jubilation in the streets of London. The nine-day reign of Queen Jane was over. She was deposed and imprisoned in the Tower of London.

The following day, Northumberland received a letter from the Council informing him that Mary was now queen and commanding him to disband his army. Northumberland knew that the game was up and did not resist. His biggest mistake, he later admitted, had been his failure to capture Mary. The following morning, the Earl of Arundel arrived to arrest Northumberland, who was carried through the streets of London to the Tower past a hostile, jeering mob. Most saw him as a power-hungry usurper who had attempted to steal the crown from the legitimate ruler. At his trial, Northumberland publicly renounced Protestantism, but this was not enough to save him, and he was executed on 22 August.

Lady Jane Grey, 'The Nine-Day Queen'.

CHAPTER FOURTEEN

Queen Mary I

Mary was greeted by cheering crowds as she rode into London on 3 August 1553. She was 37 years of age, and (discounting Jane's short, disputed reign) the first queen to rule England in her own right. Protestantism had yet to fully take root in the hearts of the English, and only a minority feared the accession of a Catholic monarch. For Mary, it had been a long and difficult road to this moment.

Born in 1516, the only surviving child of Henry VIII and Catherine of Aragon, she had grown up a princess, doted on by her parents. But her life had changed dramatically during her teenage years when Henry divorced her mother to marry Anne Boleyn. After her half-sister Elizabeth was born, Mary was forbidden access to her parents and stripped of her title of princess. She never saw her mother again. When Anne Boleyn fell, there was an opportunity for Mary to reconcile with her father, but she refused to recognize him as head of the Church.

Mary I was determined to restore England to Catholicism.

Eventually, she did submit to him, returned to court and was given a household appropriate to her status. Under the influence of Catherine Parr, Henry restored Mary to the line of succession. During Edward's reign, Mary remained for the most part on her own estates and rarely attended court. A reunion with Edward and Elizabeth over Christmas 1550 ended in embarrassment and tears for both Edward and Mary after the 13-year-old king publicly berated her for disobeying his laws and refusing to abandon Catholicism.

CONSOLIDATING POWER

The public may have been behind her, but Mary had few close allies in government. She was uncomfortably aware that almost the entire Privy Council had supported the elevation of Lady Jane Grey to the throne. They may have later changed their minds, but that had been a pragmatic decision taken once they had observed the shift in public support towards Mary.

So the new queen naturally reached out to her supporters in what remained of the conservative faction. She ordered the release of the Duke of Norfolk, Stephen Gardiner and her cousin Edward Courtenay from their cells in the Tower of London. Cardinal Reginald Pole, a senior clergyman who had been banished from England after refusing to support Henry VIII over his divorce from Catherine of Aragon, was recalled from exile. Courtenay was made Earl of Devon. Pole was made papal legate and, later, Archbishop of Canterbury. Norfolk and Gardiner were restored to their former titles and appointed to the Privy Council. Gardiner was made Lord Chancellor, and in this capacity he crowned Mary at Westminster Abbey on 1 October 1553.

Mary was sure that Lady Jane Grey, her husband Guildford Dudley and her father the Duke of Suffolk had been little more than pawns in Northumberland's scheme to retain power. She also knew she had to move cautiously until she had consolidated her own position. So instead of executing them immediately, she kept them imprisoned in the Tower. She then issued a proclamation that she would not force any of her subjects to follow her religion.

But her actions did not exactly match her words. Within months, all senior Protestant clergymen had been removed from office, to be replaced by conservatives who had been purged under Edward. Archbishop Cranmer remained in place at first, and was allowed to lead Edward's funeral service according to the rites of the new prayer book. But when, in September, Cranmer publicly proclaimed that the new doctrine was 'more pure and according to God's word, than any that hath been used in England these thousand years', he was arrested and sent to the Tower.

MARRIAGE TO PHILIP OF SPAIN

Mary was determined from the outset to undo her father's and half-brother's reforms and restore England to Catholicism. Yet she was well aware that all her plans for a Catholic reconstruction would come to nought if she allowed her Protestant half-sister Elizabeth to succeed her. To ensure her legacy, she would need a Catholic heir. Therefore, almost the first priority of her reign was to get married and have children.

Edward Courtenay and Reginald Pole were suggested as potential suitors. However, Mary soon set her sights on marrying Philip of Spain, the son of her cousin, the Holy Roman Emperor, Charles V. Philip was young and handsome, as Mary saw for herself when she was sent a portrait of him by the artist Titian. He was heir to vast territories in Europe and the New World. Yet there were problems with the match. Mary may have been queen regnant, but according English common law at that time, a woman's property and titles became her husband's upon marriage, and there was a strong fear that Philip would reign as king, relegating England to just another territory of the Habsburgs (the family of Charles V and Philip II). Even Lord Chancellor Gardiner feared the consequences and begged Mary to marry an Englishman on grounds of patriotism. But Mary's mind was made up, and she declared that 'she would choose as God inspired her'. For Philip's part, he had no feelings for Mary whatsoever, but desired the match for political and strategic reasons: an Anglo–Spanish alliance could be a powerful bulwark against France.

When the news of Mary's engagement to Philip was announced in January 1554, it provoked uprisings. A major rebellion broke out in Kent, led by Thomas Wyatt the Younger. Wyatt was a Catholic, but he had a deep fear of the Spanish state, having witnessed the Spanish Inquisition at first hand. He led 1,500 men from Rochester towards London with the aim of deposing

Mary in favour of Elizabeth. The Duke of Norfolk was dispatched to intercept him, but the duke's army proved too small, and many of its number defected to Wyatt. With 4,000 men now under his command, Wyatt entered London. Here he was met by a much stronger force of 20,000. Many of his followers deserted, and Wyatt was forced to surrender. Wyatt was tortured with the aim of extracting information about any high-ranking supporters of the rebellion. He was then beheaded at Tower Hill, and his body was quartered.

A number of senior Protestants were implicated in Wyatt's rebellion, including the Duke of Suffolk, his daughter Lady Jane Grey, her husband Guildford Dudley, Edward Courtenay and even Princess Elizabeth. Suffolk, Lady Jane and Dudley were all executed, and Courtenay was imprisoned, then exiled. Elizabeth was imprisoned in the Tower for two months, then placed under house arrest at Woodstock Palace.

To deal with people's fears about her husband-to-be, Mary consented to an act of Parliament defining the terms of their marriage. Philip was to be called 'King of England', acts of Parliament would be signed in both their names and Parliament would be called under their joint authority – *but* all of this would be for Mary's lifetime only. England would not be obliged to provide military support to Philip's father in a war, and Philip could not make decisions or appoint foreigners to office in England without Mary's consent. Although unhappy with these restrictions, Philip consented to them for the sake of the match. The couple met for the first time on 23 July 1554, and were married at Winchester Cathedral two days later. Philip could speak no English, so they conversed in a mixture of Spanish, French and Latin.

In September 1554, it was announced that the Queen was pregnant. An act of Parliament was passed making Philip regent in the event of Mary's death in childbirth. In April 1555, Elizabeth was released from house arrest so that she could witness the birth. Rumours circulated shortly afterwards that Mary had given birth to a son, prompting thanksgiving services in London, but these stories proved unfounded. The baby failed to arrive in May or June, and people began to question whether Mary was even pregnant. The Venetian ambassador, Giovanni Michieli, said the pregnancy was more likely to 'end in wind rather than anything else'. In July, there was still no baby, and the Queen's abdomen receded. It had been a false pregnancy, most likely caused by her desperate desire for a child. A grief-stricken Mary saw it as a punishment from God for her toleration of heretics in her realm. Philip was concerned that if Mary didn't produce any children, the English throne would go to Mary, Queen of Scots, who was betrothed to the Dauphin of France, Spain's chief enemy. In the interests of maintaining Habsburg influence in England, he persuaded Mary that Elizabeth should marry his cousin the Duke of Savoy. Elizabeth refused, however, and the plan came to nothing. Soon afterwards, Philip departed to lead his armies against the French in Flanders, leaving Mary in a deep depression.

Philip II was concerned that without a son the English throne would go to his mortal enemy, the Dauphin of France, by way of Mary, Queen of Scots.

RELIGION

In October 1553, at the meeting of her first Parliament, Mary began the process of restoring England to Catholicism. Under the First Statute of Repeal, the marriage of her parents was declared valid and all of Edward's religious reforms were abolished. The Six Articles of 1539 became, once again, official Church doctrine. This reaffirmed Catholic teachings on matters such as transubstantiation and clerical celibacy. Married priests were dismissed from their benefices. Mary's next challenge was to repeal her father's religious laws, including the Act of Supremacy, and restore the English Church to Rome. She met her main resistance here over the question of the status of former monastic lands sold off by Henry after the Dissolution of the Monasteries. These had been bought up by large numbers of the aristocracy and gentry, who did not take kindly to the idea that they should now voluntarily hand them back. Eventually, Mary and Pope Julius III were forced to concede that these lands could remain in the possession of their new owners.

In November 1554, Mary revived the Heresy Acts – laws dating back to the late fourteenth and early fifteenth centuries that had been repealed under Henry VIII and Edward VI. Under these laws, heresy was a religious and civil offence amounting to treason. This was a very different Mary to the new queen who had, on taking power, assured her people of religious toleration. Over the next three years, 283 Protestants were convicted of heresy and executed – most of them burned at the stake. Around 800 wealthy Protestants fled into exile, so the majority of those killed were poor and landless. However, some prominent Protestants were killed, among them the former Archbishop of Canterbury Thomas Cranmer and the Anglican bishops Hugh Latimer (Church of England chaplain to Edward VI) and Nicholas Ridley (Bishop of London).

Before he died, Cranmer recanted his Protestantism and declared that he now accepted Catholic theology, including papal supremacy and transubstantiation. Even so, Mary would not pardon him and insisted he be put to death, arguing that his sins against God were so great that mercy was not possible. On the day of his execution, Cranmer publicly withdrew his recantation and stated that the hand that had signed them would be burnt first. He then placed his right hand into the flames with the words 'that unworthy hand'. As he died, he said: 'Lord Jesus, receive my spirit … I see the heavens open and Jesus standing at the right hand of God.'

The burnings made Mary deeply unpopular, and stoked anti-Catholic and anti-Spanish sentiment. Many were deeply impressed by the bravery of the victims, prepared to martyr themselves for their Protestant faith.

WAR WITH FRANCE

However much Mary may have intended to conduct an independent foreign policy based on England's national interest, her marriage to Philip deeply influenced her deci-sion-making. In January 1556, Philip became King of Spain after his father abdicated, and he took charge of a war with France that had been in progress since 1551. In February he managed to negotiate a truce, but this soon broke down, and in March 1557 he tried to persuade Mary to support Spain by declaring war on France. Mary was happy to do so. Tensions with France had been rising since March 1556, when a French-backed plot against her had been uncovered. The plot, to invade England and overthrow Mary, had been the brainchild of Henry Dudley, son of the former regent Northumberland.

Although Mary was keen to help her husband fight the French, she met stiff opposition from her councillors, who argued that this contravened the marriage treaty. War with France, they said, was not in the national interest because it threatened French trade and, after a series of poor harvests, England lacked supplies and funds. However, another French-backed plot decided matters in favour of war. This one was led by Thomas Stafford, a nephew of Reginald Pole and a participant in Wyatt's Rebellion. In April 1557, Stafford sailed from France and landed in Scarborough with two ships and more than 30 men. He took possession of Scarborough Castle and tried to whip up a rebellion with wild talk about an imminent Spanish takeover of England. Three days later the Earl of Westmorland recaptured the castle. Stafford was arrested and subsequently executed for treason. This episode was enough to convince the Council that the French threat was serious, and in June war was declared.

At first, the war went well. With English support, the Spanish won an important victory against the French at Saint-Quentin in August 1557. However, France hit back, and in January 1558 French forces captured Calais – almost five centuries after the Norman conquest, England had lost its sole remaining possession on the European continent. The loss of Calais provoked shock and disbelief back at court, and deepened Mary's unpopularity with her people. The Queen allegedly said: 'When I am dead and cut open, they will find "Calais" engraved on my heart.'

DEATH

Philip visited England again between March and July 1557. After he left, Mary came to believe, once again, that she had fallen pregnant. As before, no child came. Instead, she grew ill, and was soon forced to accept that she was dying and Elizabeth would succeed her. The illness, which may have been ovarian cysts or uterine cancer, gave her great pain. Mary died on 17 November 1558. Her husband, who was in Brussels when he received the news, wrote to his sister: 'I felt a reasonable regret for her death.' Mary had stated in her will that she wanted to be buried alongside her mother. Instead, she was interred in Westminster Abbey. At her funeral, on 14 December, John White, Bishop of Winchester, said: 'She was a king's daughter; she was a king's sister; she was a king's wife. She was a queen, and by the same title a king also.'

Mary was the first woman to successfully claim the English throne. In many ways, she was unlucky. Her reign was blighted by poor weather and failed harvests – matters entirely beyond her control. If she had lived longer or been able to produce an heir, history might have remembered her very differently. But Mary's failures were not entirely down to ill-fortune. Her determination to marry Philip of Spain, against advice, her decision to go to war with France and the consequent loss of Calais, and her ruthless burning of Protestants all helped turn popular opinion against her and provoked a number of rebellions.

PART V: ELIZABETH I: EARLY REIGN (1558–81)

CHAPTER FIFTEEN

Domestic Policies

Princess Elizabeth was 25 years of age when she took the throne. She had already survived her fair share of scandal and danger. Her mother, Anne Boleyn, had been beheaded, and Elizabeth declared illegitimate, when she was just two years and eight months old. At 14, while living in the household of Catherine Parr, Elizabeth attracted the attention of Catherine's husband, the 39-year-old Thomas Seymour, who would often enter her bedroom in his nightgown and engage her in sexual horseplay. After Catherine died, he asked Elizabeth to marry him – the first in a long line of suitors. She turned him down, as she would all the others.

When her half-sister Mary took the throne, life for Elizabeth became a great deal more hazardous. Outwardly she conformed to the restored Catholic faith, while remaining a Protestant at heart. She tried to cultivate a low profile, yet as discontentment with Mary's reign spread, she couldn't help but become a focus for opposition. She was implicated in Wyatt's rebellion, despite protesting her innocence, and was imprisoned for two months in the Tower of London, then spent a year under house arrest at Woodstock. Several of Mary's advisors suggested that Elizabeth ought to be put on trial and executed, for, they said, Mary would never be safe while Elizabeth lived.

Through luck, and an instinct for survival, Elizabeth came through these dangerous periods in her life. After Mary's false pregnancy, life became a little easier for her as people began to accept the new political reality – that Mary was unlikely to produce an heir and Elizabeth would succeed her. By October 1558, with Mary dying, Elizabeth was already making plans for her government.

ACCESSION

Elizabeth was at her home at Hatfield House when she heard the news of her sister's death. She said: 'My lords, the law of nature moves me to sorrow for my sister; the burden that is fallen upon me makes me amazed, and yet, considering I am God's creature, ordained to obey His appointment, I will thereto yield, desiring from the bottom of my heart that I may have assistance of His grace to be the minister of His heavenly will in this office now committed to me.'

Elizabeth was crowned on 15 January 1559 in Westminster Abbey. The previous day, she had been

Elizabeth I reigned for more than four decades, during which her weak and divided country transformed itself into a significant world power.

cheered by crowds as she made her triumphal progress through the city. The event was carefully stage-managed.

She was transported in a litter covered with a cloth of gold and carried by two mules. Pageants were performed for her, several with a Protestant flavour. Looking regal in her coronation mantle and purple velvet robes, she smiled warmly at people as she passed, and responded to their good wishes. Even at this early stage, Elizabeth was taking great care with her public image.

Upon taking the throne, Elizabeth was faced by a number of difficult challenges. Mary's reign had left the country badly divided along religious lines. The economy was in a mess, and her predecessors had greatly debased the currency. England was still at war with France, and there were threats to her rule, chiefly from Catholics promoting Mary, Queen of Scots as rightful monarch.

Elizabeth appointed Sir William Cecil as her Secretary of State. Cecil, a Protestant, had been Secretary of State to Edward VI, and was already a trusted advisor to Elizabeth. In 1571, she gave him the title Lord Burghley. She was known to refer to him as her 'spirit', and she would rely greatly on his wisdom and advice throughout her reign.

RELIGIOUS SETTLEMENT

Privately, Elizabeth was a Protestant but with Catholic overtones. For example, she wore a crucifix and was never very keen on Protestant-style sermons. In terms of public policy, she was determined to find a pragmatic solution to the religious question. Her aim was to make England a Protestant nation, but in a way that would not alienate Catholics too greatly. The most conservative Catholics, she knew, would never accept anything she did, as they regarded her rule as illegitimate, and she did not even try to appease them. Neither did she take account of the reformist ideas of radical Protestants, known as Puritans. Instead, she tried to forge a settlement that would appeal to the large majority of moderates in both camps.

Parliament was summoned in 1559 to debate legislation that would restore much of the Protestant settlement of Edward VI. The new bill sought to recreate an independent Church of England and re-introduce Protestant theology. The heresy laws were to be repealed; the Book of Common Prayer was to be brought back into use; priests would be allowed to marry; images would be banned from churches; and Catholic doctrine on matters such as transubstantiation was to be rejected.

The House of Commons supported the proposals, but there was opposition from the Lords, especially from the bishops. Compromises were made. The Book of Common Prayer was adapted to allow clergymen to wear priestly vestments. Instead of 'Supreme Head of the Church of England', the title her father adopted, Elizabeth would be called 'Supreme Governor of the Church of England', to mollify those who could not accept the idea of a woman as leader of the Church.

The new religious settlement was enshrined in two acts of Parliament, passed in 1559 – the Act of Supremacy and the Act of Uniformity. Under the Act of Supremacy, all clergymen were obliged to swear an oath of loyalty to the monarch as the supreme governor, or risk removal from office. The Act of Uniformity made church attendance and the use of the Book of Common Prayer compulsory. Yet penalties for failure to do so were not too harsh. The Elizabethan religious settlement is commonly regarded as the end point of the English Reformation and the foundation of modern Anglicanism.

THE POOR LAWS

One of the major challenges facing Elizabeth on the domestic front was an increase in poverty and vagrancy, leading to a rise in civil disorder. There were several reasons for this. One was the breakdown of the medieval feudal system, under which the landed aristocracy were responsible for the peasants who lived on their land. The end of feudalism meant greater social mobility for ordinary people, but also an increase in poverty.

Henry VIII's Dissolution of the Monasteries also had profound social effects, casting thousands of monks and nuns, as well as those who worked for them, into destitution and homelessness. An important role of the monasteries had been charitable work, feeding and clothing the hungry and helping the sick. The disappearance of these institutions meant the loss of an essential safety net for the poor and vulnerable.

Changes to agriculture were also to blame. Wool was becoming a major English export during Tudor times, and landowners were consequently turning their fields over to sheep-rearing. These land enclosures threatened the livelihoods of rural people who for centuries had grown their crops and grazed their animals on what they regarded as common land. The new, larger, pastoral farms required fewer labourers, causing a rise in rural unemployment.

In 1563, Elizabeth's government passed the Poor Law. The law distinguished between different types of poor people as a way of determining what treatment they should receive. The 'deserving poor' were the old, the young and the sick who were poor through no fault of their own. They were to be provided with 'outdoor relief' in the form of clothes, food and money. The sick were cared for in hospitals, and apprenticeships were arranged for the young. The 'deserving unemployed' were the able-bodied who were unable to find employment. They were provided with 'indoor relief' – given shelter and employment in almshouses and workhouses. The 'undeserving poor' were the able-bodied who had turned to a life of crime or vagrancy. Punishments for the undeserving poor could be very harsh, including beatings, imprisonment and even hanging.

Further laws were passed in 1572 and 1576. The 1572 act made alleviation of poverty the responsibility of each local parish. The justice of the peace of the parish was allowed to collect a weekly tax called the Poor Rate from local landowners, and the revenue was used to help the deserving poor. Anyone refusing to pay could be imprisoned. The 1576 act provided for the establishment of workhouses, or poorhouses, in every town, as well as 'houses of correction' for vagrants and beggars.

ROYAL PROGRESSES

Throughout her reign, Elizabeth undertook journeys around her kingdom. These 'royal progresses' usually took place in summer, keeping her out of London during the plague season. They allowed the Queen to see her subjects and be seen by them. At each stage of her journey she would stay at the house of a noble, where she expected to be entertained in style. This could be extremely expensive for the host, for on a typical progress Elizabeth was accompanied by at least a hundred members of her household, all of whom had to be housed and fed.

An account from the year 1564 describes a royal progress that stopped for five days in Cambridge. As the Queen entered the city gates, preceded by trumpets and followed by her magnificent retinue, she was welcomed by all the scholars of the university, kneeling and calling out '*Vivat Regina!*' For the next five days, the Queen was entertained by a series of ceremonies, entertainments and 'scholastic exercises'. She visited the colleges founded by members of the Tudor family, attended lectures and Latin plays, listened to orations and disputes and was presented with numerous gifts. She also gave several speeches of her own in Latin. When she finally left, one day later than planned, she said she would have stayed even longer 'if provision of beer and ale' could have been made for her court.

CHAPTER SIXTEEN

Foreign Policy and the Marriage Question

During the early part of her reign, Elizabeth pursued a mainly cautious and defensive foreign policy. The only aggressive move she made was to send troops to occupy Le Havre, on the French coast, in October 1562. In May of that year, Huguenots (French Protestants) had captured the city, looted churches and expelled Catholics. They then appealed to the English for help in defending it against the inevitable counterattack by the forces of the French king, Charles IX. Elizabeth agreed, thinking that Le Havre could replace Calais as an English-controlled port on the Continental mainland. But after a prolonged siege by French troops, the English were finally expelled at the end of July 1563.

ANGLO–SPANISH RELATIONS

Rivalry between the Habsburgs and France, as well as competition for Elizabeth's hand in marriage (see pages 136-7), kept England relatively safe for much of the 1560s and '70s. Relations with Spain, in contrast, grew steadily worse during this period. One reason for this was the Dutch Revolt against Philip of Spain. The rebellion in the Spanish-controlled Netherlands had been building since the mid-1550s, and flared up in 1566 due to Dutch anger at the heavy burden of taxation, centralized rule and the suppression of Protestantism. Philip responded by sending a large force of Spanish and Italian troops to the Netherlands. The rebellion was ruthlessly crushed, and large taxes were levied to pay for the army of occupation. The Dutch rebels turned to Elizabeth for help.

Elizabeth responded cautiously. She disliked the idea of Spanish armies in the Netherlands, yet neither did she wish to do anything that could provoke open war with Spain. So, during the 1570s, she lent small sums of money to the Dutch rebels and allowed English volunteer soldiers to go to their aid, without ever committing any of her own troops. In 1579, the situation resolved itself, at least temporarily, when the Netherlands split in two: the northern provinces became independent, while the southern provinces remained loyal to Spain.

Another major reason for the decline in Anglo–Spanish relations was the actions of English privateers in the Spanish Main (the Caribbean coast of Latin America), and for this Elizabeth did bear a great deal of responsibility. Spain had established colonies in the Caribbean and along the coasts of South America. From here they shipped gold, silver, precious gems and spices back to Spain. These treasure fleets were frequently attacked by English seamen, using the Caribbean islands as their bases, who were essentially licenced pirates. Elizabeth's government issued them with 'letters of marque', authorizing them to plunder Spanish ships. This suited Elizabeth, as it allowed her to attack the enemy, Spain, without officially declaring war. Also, the privateers would offer a proportion of their booty to the Queen, enriching the royal treasury. The most famous of them were Francis Drake, Walter Raleigh, Richard Hawkins, John Hawkins, Martin Frobisher, Humphrey Gilbert and Richard Grenville.

Famously, Drake circumnavigated the globe in 1577–80 in his ship the *Golden Hinde*. The Spanish, who had taken steps to protect their Atlantic sea lanes from privateering, were amazed by Drake's unexpected appearance on the Pacific coast of South America, and he was able to net an enormous haul of treasure. He and his crew became popular folk heroes back in England.

THE MARRIAGE QUESTION

As soon as Elizabeth became queen, one question was uppermost in everyone's minds: whom would she marry? She was the last of the Tudor line, and to avoid political instability and possibly civil war when she died, it was considered essential for her to produce an heir. Elizabeth was young, unlike Mary, and many hoped that England would soon have a royal family again.

Elizabeth was certainly a desirable marriage partner, with a number of European monarchs eager to secure England as an ally. During the early weeks of her reign, ambassadors from the great royal houses pressed the suits of their masters and their masters' relatives. Offers of marriage came from King Philip II of Spain, Prince Eric of Sweden, Archduke Charles of the Holy Roman Empire, the son of the Duke of Saxony and the Earl of Arran. She had English suitors, too, including the Earl of Arundel and Sir William Pickering.

Elizabeth politely refused the offer from the King of Spain, while allowing the other suitors to remain hopeful as her advisors examined the pros and cons of each potential match. Whether she ever actually intended to marry is an open question. A clue to her feelings may be found in a remark she made in 1563: 'If I follow the inclination of my nature, it is this: beggar-woman and single, far rather than queen and married.' She may have been dissuaded from the idea of marriage by the experience of Mary, who had allowed her husband Philip to influence English foreign policy. Any husband of royal status would probably wish to rule as an equal partner, and neither Elizabeth nor her ministers had any desire to cede even partial control of English affairs to a foreign king. Particularly problematic was the fact that several of her suitors, including Philip of Spain and Archduke Charles, were Catholic.

DUDLEY

One man Elizabeth might have been inclined to marry was her childhood friend Lord Robert Dudley, now her Master of Horse. By 1559, she was deeply in love with her 'Bonny Sweet Robin', as she called him. Dudley was one of the few men who, she believed, loved her for herself and not because she was Queen of England. But Dudley was already married, to a young woman called Amy Robsart. Also, he was the son of the much-reviled Duke of Northumberland and suspected of involvement in his father's scheme to place Lady Jane Grey on the throne. Nevertheless, Elizabeth remained stubbornly enamoured of him, and rumours soon began to circulate that Dudley was going to annul his marriage or even kill his wife in order to marry the Queen.

So when, in September 1560, Amy Robsart was found dead at the bottom of a narrow staircase with her neck broken, suspicions were immediately raised that this was no tragic accident but foul murder. A subsequent inquest concluded that Robsart's death was an accident. Even so, Elizabeth's advisors told her she must forget all about marrying Dudley, who was now tainted by the gossip, regardless of his guilt or innocence in the affair. Yet she continued to entertain the possibility of marrying him, and he remained the most serious contender for her hand for the next 10 years. Even after that, she continued to express jealousy towards his mistresses, and when he remarried in 1578, Elizabeth reacted with anger and developed an abiding hatred of his wife.

Anjou

The final and most significant political courtship of Elizabeth's reign was with Francis, Duke of Alençon, later Duke of Anjou, the brother of the French king. By 1569 relations with the Habsburgs had deteriorated and England needed France as an ally. The courtship continued from 1572 to 1581, and for a time Elizabeth appeared to take it seriously, even though he was not particularly handsome and bore the scars of an attack of smallpox. She called Anjou her 'Frog', and wore a frog-shaped earring that he had sent her. Although the French were Catholic, they did not appear to be as hostile to Protestantism as the Spanish were, and Anjou himself was known to be sympathetic towards the Huguenots. Elizabeth's courtiers were divided over whether marriage to Anjou would be a good thing. Many feared a takeover by the French; others, including Lord Burghley, were strongly in favour of the match. In the end, the courtship came to nothing. By this time, Elizabeth was in her late forties and could no longer realistically expect to bear a child or therefore to use marriage as a diplomatic weapon.

Marriage, diplomacy and the Virgin Queen

For over 20 years, Elizabeth played the 'marriage game', and it became an important tool of diplomacy. Whenever

England needed powerful friends, all the Queen had to do was hold out the possibility of marriage. The bait was impossible to resist, and she could be assured of support from one country or another for as long as she needed it. Thus there were times when both Eric of Sweden and Archduke Charles had high hopes for her hand. Her ministers, while acknowledging the effectiveness of this tactic, became impatient, especially after she suffered an attack of smallpox in 1563 that came close to killing her.

Shortly after her twenty-ninth birthday, Elizabeth began running a high fever and smallpox was diagnosed. Within a couple of days she had lapsed into a coma. She awoke 48 hours later, very weak, and thus she remained for a time, drifting in and out of consciousness. Meanwhile, the Privy Council conducted an urgent debate about the succession. One group favoured Lady Katherine Grey, younger sister of the ill-fated Jane. Another supported the Earl of Huntingdon, a descendant of Edward II, with no close blood ties to Elizabeth. In a moment of lucidity, Elizabeth appointed Dudley as Lord Protector of England. Her councillors pretended to agree to this, believing her 'all but gone'. Privately, they decided such an appointment would lead to civil war.

To everyone's great relief, Elizabeth slowly recovered from her illness. Yet the episode was a frightening reminder of the chaos that could ensue if their sovereign died without a named successor. Her councillors urged her to marry or nominate an heir to prevent civil war upon her death. Elizabeth refused to do either. In some ways, her silence on the issue strengthened her own political security. If she named a successor, that person could become an unwitting figurehead for rebellions, much as she herself had been during Mary's reign.

In 1559, Elizabeth told Parliament: 'And, in the end, this shall be for me sufficient, that a marble stone shall declare that a queen, having reigned such a time, lived and died a virgin.' She did not have to wait for a tombstone inscription. In her own lifetime, her unmarried status inspired a cult of virginity, with poets and painters depicting her as a virgin or a goddess or both. In 1578, people expressed their opposition to the marriage negotiations with the Duke of Anjou by paying public tribute to their Virgin Queen.

CHAPTER SEVENTEEN

Mary, Queen of Scots

Elizabeth faced a strong rival claim to her throne from her Catholic cousin, Mary, Queen of Scots. Mary, born in 1542, was the daughter of James V of Scotland and his French wife, Mary of Guise. Her paternal grandmother was Margaret Tudor, sister of Henry VIII. To Catholics, who had never accepted the legitimacy of Henry VIII's marriage to Anne Boleyn, Mary, Queen of Scots was the rightful ruler of England.

THE YOUNG QUEEN

When Mary was just a few days old, her father died and the infant girl was crowned Queen of Scotland, with the Earl of Arran appointed as regent. Henry VIII tried and failed to force a match between Mary and his son Edward, and Mary was sent to France to marry the dauphin, Francis, who later became King Francis II. In 1559, 15-year-old Francis inherited the throne when his father,

Henry II, was killed in a jousting accident. Mary, his 16-year-old wife, found herself queen of both France and Scotland. By now, Mary's mother was regent of Scotland, aided by French troops. The French presence in Scotland alarmed the newly enthroned Elizabeth, as did the fact that the crowns of England's two traditional enemies were now united. She feared that the French would invade England and try to place Mary, Queen of Scots on the throne.

Mary, Queen of Scots was a Catholic monarch in a time when her homeland was beset by Protestant rebellion.

Fortunately for Elizabeth, however, Mary of Guise's position in Scotland was fragile. Scottish Protestants were challenging her rule, and she was clinging on to power with the help of the French troops. Elizabeth's advisors urged her to support the Scottish rebels, but Elizabeth was reluctant to assist an insurgency that sought the overthrow of a sovereign ruler. In the end she agreed to send in some troops, but the intervention was ineptly led and resulted in a humiliating defeat for English forces. However, William Cecil retrieved the situation by travelling to Scotland and negotiating the Treaty of Edinburgh, guaranteeing peace between the two realms and removing the French troops from Scotland. Mary of Guise died in June 1560, a month before the treaty was signed. Her daughter, still in France, refused to ratify it or relinquish her claim to the English throne.

RETURN TO SCOTLAND

In August 1561, after the death of her young husband, Mary was forced to return to the land of her birth to take up the reins of power. When she arrived at Leith, crowds were there to welcome their long-absent monarch. Accustomed to the luxury and splendour of the French court, Mary found Scotland austere. More troublingly for her, by this time the country had an established Protestant church and was run by a council of Protestant nobles supported by Elizabeth. To their chagrin, Mary again refused to sign the Treaty of Edinburgh. Nevertheless, she did her best to govern what was now a largely Protestant realm, tolerating the new religion while remaining a Catholic in private. Like Elizabeth, she faced immediate pressure to marry and produce an heir. Elizabeth suggested she marry Robert Dudley. The English queen knew that Dudley would always be loyal to her, and she thought that this might be a way of guaranteeing peace between the two kingdoms. Elizabeth even dared hope that their child could one day, with her blessing, inherit both English and Scottish thrones. To make Dudley a more suitable match for a queen, Elizabeth elevated him to the peerage in 1564, making him Earl of Leicester. Mary, however, was insulted by the suggestion, as Dudley was widely rumoured to be Elizabeth's lover and a wife-murderer to boot. To Dudley's great relief, Mary turned him down.

MARRIAGE TO DARNLEY

In February 1565, Mary was visited by Henry Stuart, Lord Darnley, her English Catholic cousin. Darnley's maternal grandmother was Margaret Tudor, so he too had a claim to the English throne. Mary was attracted to him physically, and he seemed in every way a suitable match. In July 1565, they were married. Elizabeth was greatly disturbed by this development: with their joint claim to the throne, the couple would be able to attract substantial support in any bid to depose her.

But Mary's marriage to Darnley soon proved to be a disastrous mistake – the first of a series that would ultimately lead to her downfall. He turned out to be a vain, arrogant and unstable man with a violent temper made worse by his drinking. To his fury, Mary refused to grant him the Crown Matrimonial, which would have made him successor to the throne if she died childless. A month after their wedding, Mary became pregnant, and rumours flew around that the father was not Darnley but her private secretary, David Rizzio, to whom she had become very close. One evening in March 1566, Darnley and his friends stabbed Rizzio to death in front of the seven-months-pregnant Mary. It was a horrific attack – Rizzio received 56 stab wounds. English diplomats, reporting the incident to Elizabeth, said it was part of Darnley's attempt to force Mary to offer him the Crown Matrimonial.

Darnley publicly denied involvement in the murder, and Mary remained silent on the matter. Yet suspicions soon centred on him, and he became a hated figure in Scotland. Mary now feared and distrusted her husband, and the couple separated. On 19 June 1566, their son was born – the future James VI of Scotland and James I of England. Eight months later, Darnley was killed after a suspicious explosion at his residence, although his cause of death appeared to be from strangulation.

MARRIAGE TO BOTHWELL

Among those accused of Darnley's murder was James Hepburn, Earl of Bothwell, a prominent Scottish nobleman and close friend of Mary's. Not long afterwards, in May 1567, Mary married Bothwell, prompting speculation that she had conspired with him to murder Darnley. Elizabeth wrote to her: 'How could a worse choice be made for your honour than in such haste to marry such a subject, who besides other and notorious lacks, public fame has charged with the murder of your late husband, besides the touching of yourself also in some part, though we trust in that behalf falsely.'

The Scottish people were outraged by the marriage. Twenty-six Scottish nobles, known as the Confederate Lords, raised an army in revolt against Mary. They met at Carberry Hill on 15 June, where Mary and Bothwell's forces melted away at the sight of the Lords' army; Bothwell was driven into exile, while Mary was imprisoned in Loch Leven Castle. On 24 July she was forced to abdicate in favour of her one-year-old son, James, who would be raised as a Protestant. Mary's half-brother, James Stewart, Earl of Moray, became regent.

MARY IN ENGLAND

In 1568, Mary escaped from Loch Leven and managed to raise an army of 6,000. But she was defeated by Moray's forces, and fled south into England, where she had once been assured of support by Elizabeth. Mary expected her cousin to help her regain the throne, and this was indeed Elizabeth's first instinct – the forced abdication of a fellow monarch set a dangerous precedent, and she feared what it meant for her own position. But after discussing the matter with her councillors, Elizabeth decided it would be safest to detain Mary in England. She would 'take her under her protection' – which in practice meant imprisoning her – and for the next 19 years, Mary was held in various English castles. Many of Elizabeth's councillors urged her to execute Mary, fearing that she would become a focus for rebellion, but for a long time Elizabeth resisted such calls.

RISING OF THE NORTH

The councillors' fears were by no means unfounded. In 1569, Catholic nobles in the north of England rose up in rebellion – their plan being to release Mary, marry her to Thomas Howard, Duke of Norfolk, and install her on the English throne. The rebel earls occupied Durham, then Barnard Castle. From there they marched to Clifford Moor, but found little popular support. On 13 December, they were confronted by a royal army under the Earl of Sussex. The rebel earls retreated, dispersed their armies and fled into Scotland. One of them, the Earl of Northumberland, was captured and executed, as were some 600 of his supporters. Norfolk managed to avoid implication in the rebellion, but was nevertheless imprisoned in the Tower.

Pope Pius V, unaware that the rebellion had been crushed, issued a papal bull entitled *Regnans in Excelsis* ('Reigning on High'), which declared that 'Elizabeth, the

pretended Queen of England and the servant of crime'
was a heretic. The bull released all her subjects from any
allegiance to her and threatened to excommunicate any
Catholic who obeyed her orders. *Regnans in Excelsis*
unnerved Elizabeth and her councillors, and hardened
their attitude towards rebellious Catholics. It also inspired
many of these rebels to continue plotting to place Mary
on the English throne.

THE RIDOLFI PLOT

Shortly after the failed northern rebellion, a Florentine
banker called Roberto Ridolfi began work on a new plot
to overthrow Elizabeth. The plan was to raise an army
in the Netherlands under the command of the Duke of
Alba, invade England, foment a rebellion in the north
and, as before, marry Mary to the Duke of Norfolk and
place her on the throne. Elizabeth's intelligence network
uncovered the Ridolfi Plot in April 1571, before the
invasion could be launched. Through confessions
extracted under torture, government agents learned that
both Norfolk and Mary were deeply involved in the plot.
Elizabeth had Norfolk beheaded, but spared Mary –
though never again would she contemplate restoring
Mary to the Scottish throne.

PART VI: ELIZABETH I: LATE REIGN (1581–1603)

CHAPTER EIGHTEEN

The Babington Plot

The 1580s were very dangerous years for Elizabeth and her government, with Catholics at home and on the Continent actively plotting the Queen's overthrow. Her Secretary of State and 'spymaster' during this period was Francis Walsingham, who worked closely with Elizabeth's chief advisor Lord Burghley (Lord High Treasurer from 1572) to promote England's interests at home and overseas, undermine her enemies and foil numerous plots against the Queen. Having witnessed at first hand the 1572 St Barthomew's Massacre of Huguenots (Protestants) in France, Walsingham was driven by a Protestant zeal to counter Catholicism, and he had no qualms about using torture against suspected conspirators, including priests. Walsingham viewed Mary, Queen of Scots as a dangerous woman and would have liked, if Elizabeth had allowed it, to have her executed. In January 1572, he wrote to Burghley: 'so long as that devilish woman lives, neither Her Majesty must make account to continue in quiet possession of her crown nor her faithful servants assure themselves of safety of their lives.'

THE THROCKMORTON PLOT

The first significant plot of the 1580s was led by Sir Francis Throckmorton, a cousin of Elizabeth Throckmorton, the Queen's first lady-in-waiting. The plan was to overthrow the Elizabethan regime by the careful co-ordination of three separate actions: the assassination of Queen Elizabeth; an invasion of England led by Henry I, Duke of Guise, financed by Spain and the Pope; and a simultaneous uprising by English Catholics.

Throckmorton hatched the conspiracy while meeting with exiled English Catholics in Europe. On his return to London in 1583, he met secretly with Bernardino de Mendoza, the Spanish ambassador. Throckmorton became the intermediary between Mary, Queen of Scots, Mendoza and several other conspirators. Walsingham soon became suspicious and placed Throckmorton under surveillance. After six months, Throckmorton was arrested, and incriminating documents in his possession were seized. He and several co-conspirators were imprisoned in the Tower. Mendoza was expelled from the country – he would be the last Spanish ambassador at Elizabeth's court. Under torture, Throckmorton revealed the full extent of the plot; he was convicted of high treason and executed in July 1584.

In the wake of the Throckmorton Plot, Burghley and Walsingham drafted a document called the Bond of

Association. This obliged all signatories to hunt down and execute anyone who attempted to usurp the throne or assassinate the Queen. The document also stated that if anyone plotted against the Queen on behalf of someone in the line of succession, then the person in the line of succession would be excluded from the line and executed. In other words, Mary, Queen of Scots could be executed if a plot to put her on the throne was discovered – even if she had not initiated the plot.

Hundreds of English nobles, including the entire Privy Council, signed the Bond of Association. It was also signed, under pressure, by Mary, Queen of Scots. Walsingham and Burghley hoped, by means of the Bond of Association, to pressure Elizabeth into signing Mary's death warrant the next time there was a plot to put her on the throne. They realized, however, that the only way to ensure Elizabeth's signature on such a warrant would be if they could produce physical evidence of Mary's involvement in the plot. So they set their spies to the task of sniffing out new conspiracies. Their aim, this time, wasn't simply to foil the plot, but to lure Mary into giving it her written support and encouragement – entrapment, in other words.

Following the Throckmorton Plot, Elizabeth wished to tighten the security around Mary. So, in 1585, Mary was moved under heavy guard from her residence at Tutbury Castle to the more stoutly defended and prison-like environment of Chartley Castle in Staffordshire. Here she was kept strictly confined under the supervision of Sir Amias Paulet, a Puritan who abhorred the Catholic faith. For good measure, Elizabeth banned Mary from any correspondence with the outside world. This posed a problem for Walsingham, because if Mary was barred from communicating, how was he supposed to entrap her in another plot? The solution to this problem, he realized, would be to find a secret method by which Mary could communicate with her supporters – and then, with the help of a double agent, intercept the messages.

THE DOUBLE AGENT

Through his spies, Walsingham already knew the whereabouts of a number of enemy agents on the Continent, including one Thomas Morgan, a confidant of Mary, Queen of Scots, based in Paris. So when Morgan was visited in October 1585 by a young English Catholic named Gilbert Gifford, Walsingham's suspicions were raised. On Gifford's return to England in December, Walsingham had him arrested and brought to him for questioning. In the course of the interrogation, Walsingham convinced Gifford to work for him as a double agent.

With Gifford's help, Walsingham soon became aware of a new plot against Elizabeth. In March 1586, an English Jesuit priest named John Ballard met with several conspirators, including Gifford, and together formed a plan to assassinate Elizabeth, solicit a Spanish invasion of England and install Mary on the throne. Soon afterwards, Ballard recruited Anthony Babington, a young Catholic noble. Babington had been devoted to Mary ever since he had served as page to one of Mary's earlier jailors, the Earl of Shrewsbury. Ballard asked Babington to lead and organize English Catholics in an uprising against Elizabeth. Babington was initially reluctant, until Ballard assured him that plans were already in place for the assassination of Elizabeth, and that a force of some 60,000 men under the Duke of Guise stood ready to invade England.

Walsingham, who was aware of all or most of this, could have foiled the plot at any time he chose, but he was determined this time to wait until he had ensnared Mary as well. To this end, he placed Gifford close to Mary, inside Chartley Castle. Gifford was able to win Mary's trust by showing her a letter of introduction from Thomas Morgan, whom Mary knew well. He then explained to Mary a secret communication system that had been set up so that she could correspond with her supporters. A local beer brewer had agreed to act as facilitator. The brewer would move messages in and out of Chartley by placing them in a watertight casing inserted within the cork of a beer barrel.

Of course, this elaborate scheme had been worked out by Walsingham with the full knowledge of Mary's jailor, Paulet. Once everything had been set up, Gifford approached the French ambassador to England, Baron de Châteauneuf-sur-Cher, and gave him details of the secret communication system without letting on that it was actually being operated by Walsingham. He asked Châteauneuf to initiate the correspondence by writing the first letter to Mary. The letter would contain the key to a cipher (supplied to him by Walsingham via Gifford), so that Mary could write her letters in code, and decipher the letters she received. Thereafter, all correspondence between Mary and her supporters would go through Châteauneuf.

Walsingham placed another agent called Thomas Phelippes in Chartley Castle. Phelippes was a cipher and language expert. His job would be to receive any letter going to or from Mary, decode it and send a copy to Walsingham. The letter would then be resealed and given back to Gifford, who would pass it to the brewer, who would send it on to either Mary or Châteauneuf.

THE FATAL CORRESPONDENCE

On 7 July 1586, Anthony Babington sent a coded letter to Mary via Châteauneuf. Phelippes decoded it. The letter contained full details of the plot. Babington told Mary about the plans for a foreign invasion; an insurrection by English Catholics; a six-man assassination team to murder Elizabeth; and his own intention to lead a rescue party to deliver Mary safely from Chartley. Mary received the letter on 14 July, and three days later she replied to Babington. In the course of her long letter, she praised him on all aspects of the plot; advised him on how to effect a successful rescue; expressed support for the assassination of Elizabeth; and stressed the necessity of a Spanish invasion of England. On 19 July, Phelippes decoded the letter and sent a copy to Walsingham with a small picture of a gallows on its seal. The letter was everything Walsingham had hoped for.

In early August, all the conspirators were arrested. On 20 September, Ballard and Babington were hanged, drawn and quartered. The horrific nature of these executions caused such public revulsion that Elizabeth relented slightly – the remaining conspirators were allowed to hang until dead before being disembowelled.

In October 1586, Mary was put on trial at Fotheringhay Castle in Northamptonshire, with 46 English nobles sitting in judgement. Mary was not allowed legal counsel; nor was she able to review the evidence against her or provide witnesses to speak on her behalf. The trial was, of course, a foregone conclusion with just one of the judges voting 'not guilty'. As she was Queen of Scotland, Mary was found guilty of treason against the foreign country of England. Even at this stage, Elizabeth hesitated to sentence her cousin to death, fearful of the dangerous precedent it would set. Finally, under pressure from the Privy Council, Parliament and the general public, she signed Mary's death warrant on 1 February 1587. She entrusted the warrant to William Davison, junior secretary of state. A week later, in front of 300 witnesses, Mary was executed by beheading. On hearing of the execution, Elizabeth claimed not to have ordered it, saying she hadn't meant Davison to pass on the warrant. Davison was arrested and imprisoned in the Tower. He was released in October 1588 on the orders of Burghley and Walsingham.

The Queen, laying herself down on the Ground, and stretching forth her Neck on the Block, repeats many times, "Into thy Hands, O Lord, do I commit my Spirit."

Mary, Queen of Scots had, in the minds of many Catholics, a strong claim to the English throne – but she made a series of miscalculations and ultimately lost her life.

Chapter Nineteen

Foreign Affairs

The second half of Elizabeth's reign was mostly taken up with a long undeclared war with Spain. Her later years also witnessed an expensive war in Ireland. At the same time, English explorers such as Sir Martin Frobisher and John Davies searched for a North-West or North-East Passage – a route to the East Indies (and access to the lucrative spice trade) that did not involve sailing around the Horn of Africa. Attempts were made to found English colonies in the New World, in Newfoundland (1583) and on Roanoke Island in present-day North Carolina (1585–91). Both failed, but lessons were learned from these experiments that led to the establishment of successful English colonies in the seventeenth century. The later Elizabethan era also saw an expansion of trade beyond Europe. The Turkey Company (later the Levant Company) was formed in 1581 to trade in currants, wine, cotton and silk from the Eastern Mediterranean. In 1585, Elizabeth granted a monopoly to the Barbary Company to trade in sugar from the Barbary Coast (present-day Morocco). And in 1600, the East India Company was founded to compete with Spain and Portugal for control of the spice trade. It would go on to become the biggest company in the world.

THE CONFLICT WITH SPAIN

Since 1558, many senior members of the court of King Philip of Spain had dreamed of the *Empresa de Inglaterra* ('Enterprise of England') – an invasion of England to overthrow the Protestant regime. However, the plan had only ever received half-hearted support from the King. He knew all about English naval power, having initiated a naval rebuilding programme while married to Mary. Moreover, without a firm base in the Netherlands, any armada would have to be launched from Spain – a very risky enterprise. On the other hand, English support for Dutch rebels in the Spanish Netherlands, as well as attacks on the Spanish treasure fleet by English privateers, had gradually ratcheted up tensions between the two countries and encouraged Philip to think again about the *Empresa*.

In the end, it was a crisis in the Netherlands that tipped Anglo–Spanish hostility into outright war. In 1584, Alexander Farnese, the Duke of Parma and governor of the Spanish Netherlands, began a military campaign to take control of the United Provinces – the independent, Protestant provinces of the northern

Netherlands. Town after town fell to his forces – Tournai, Maastricht, Breda, Bruges and Ghent all opened their gates. Elizabeth watched with growing alarm at this expansion of Spanish power so close to England's shores. In August 1585, the city of Antwerp fell to Parma's army, giving the Spanish a major port from which to launch an invasion of England. Elizabeth felt compelled to act. She signed the Treaty of Nonsuch with the United Provinces. Under its terms, she agreed to send a military force, together with funds, to help the Dutch. Philip II considered the treaty a declaration of war by Elizabeth, and this marked the beginning of a conflict that would last, on and off, until 1604.

In December 1585, Robert Dudley, the Earl of Leicester, arrived in the Netherlands with a force of about 7,000 men. Elizabeth, in characteristically cautious style, did not intend the English expeditionary force to actually engage decisively with the enemy. She saw it as a way of superficially honouring the terms of her treaty with the Dutch, and as a bargaining tool once she began secret peace talks with the Spanish.

Unfortunately for her, Dudley did not see things this way, and he duly embarked on a full-blooded military campaign. To Elizabeth's fury, he accepted the post of governor-general of the United Provinces. During the treaty negotiations, Elizabeth had specifically rejected this title, offered to her by the Dutch, because she wanted to avoid further antagonizing the Spanish. She sent

Dudley a letter expressing her outrage. On her insistence, this was read out before the Dutch Council of State, which was a humiliation for Dudley and severely undermined his authority among the Dutch. The ensuing campaign turned out to be an expensive failure, thanks to Elizabeth's repeated refusal to send more funds, Dudley's incompetence as a military leader and the divided, factional nature of the Dutch leadership. Dudley resigned his command in December 1587.

THE SPANISH ARMADA

The English intervention in the Netherlands was the final straw for Philip, and from early 1586 he began building a large navy to attack England – the *Empresa* was finally under way. Philip's plan was for the fleet to bring troops from Spain to secure a beachhead in Kent, before ferrying troops from the Netherlands. Through their spy networks, Burghley and Walsingham were able to learn something of Spanish plans. Sir Francis Drake, England's foremost sailor, was dispatched to Spain to carry out a pre-emptive strike against Philip. In April 1587, Drake sailed into the harbour at Cádiz and set fire to 37 Spanish ships. The raid delayed but did not put an end to the *Empresa*.

The Spanish Armada, a great fleet of 122 ships conveying an army of 26,000 soldiers and sailors, set sail from Lisbon on 12 July 1588 under the command of the Duke of Medina Sidonia. A further 30,000 troops, under the Duke of Parma, awaited the Armada's arrival in the Spanish Netherlands. The English made an attempt to intercept it in the Bay of Biscay, but were blown back by storms. Delayed by bad weather, the Armada finally arrived off Land's End on 19 July. The English fleet was caught by surprise while it was being resupplied in Plymouth Harbour. The tide was in the Spaniards' favour, and Medina Sidonia's military advisors urged him to attack the fleet and then start the invasion from Plymouth. But Medina Sidonia decided against this, because Philip had forbidden them to invade until they had picked up Parma's troops. The Armada continued its journey east along the Channel. When the tide turned, 55 English ships emerged from Plymouth Harbour and gave chase, bombarding the Spanish ships from a distance with cannon fire. They were too far away to cause much damage, but two Spanish ships sank when they collided.

On 27 July, the Armada anchored off Calais. This gave the English the opportunity to launch a fire-ship attack. The fire ships spread panic among the Spanish fleet, and most of its ships cut their anchor cables and scattered. No Spanish ships were burnt, but the disciplined formation of the Armada had been broken. The English engaged them at Gravelines, sinking five Spanish ships in an eight-hour battle. Strong winds then blew the Armada into the North Sea. Medina Sidonia had no choice but to continue northwards and chart a risky course home around Scotland and then south past the west coast of Ireland. Many ships were lost on the voyage, battered by powerful winds off the coasts of Scotland and Ireland. In the end, just 67 ships and fewer than 10,000 men made it back to Spain.

The English, unaware of the fate of the Armada, continued their preparations for defence against an invasion from the Spanish Netherlands. A force of 4,000 soldiers was stationed at West Tilbury in Essex under the command of Robert Dudley. He invited Elizabeth to come and inspect them, which she did on 9 August. Wearing a silver breastplate over a white velvet dress, she addressed the troops in one of her most famous speeches:

My loving people, we have been persuaded by some that are careful of our safety, to take heed how we commit ourself to armed multitudes for fear of treachery; but I assure you, I do not desire to live to distrust my faithful and loving people. Let tyrants fear, I have always so behaved myself, that under God I have placed my chiefest strength and safeguard in the loyal hearts and goodwill of my subjects; and, therefore, I am come amongst you as you see at this time, not for my recreation and disport, but being resolved, in the midst and heat of battle, to live or die amongst you all – to lay down for my God, and for my kingdoms, and for my people, my honour and my blood even in the dust. I know I have the body of a weak and feeble woman, but I have the heart and stomach of a king, and of a King of England too, and think foul scorn that Parma or Spain, or any Prince of Europe should dare to invade the borders of my realm.

Once it became clear that the Armada had been defeated, the nation rejoiced. Cheering crowds lined the streets as Elizabeth processed to a thanksgiving service at St Paul's Cathedral. This was a victory not only for Elizabeth but also for the idea of a Protestant England, and for the English it was seen as a sign of God's favour.

The Spanish Armada threatened an invasion of England until a fire-ship attack near Calais badly damaged the fleet in July 1588.

THE CONTINUING CONFLICT

The defeat of the Spanish Armada did not end the conflict with Spain, which would rumble on inconclusively for another 16 years. The Spanish rebuilt their fleet, and the English continued to live in fear of invasion right through the 1590s. The theatre of war widened from 1589, as England and Spain clashed in France and, later, Ireland.

In 1589, the English sent their own armada to Spain under the command of Sir Francis Drake and Sir John Norreys. The plan was to destroy the Spanish Atlantic navy, which was being refitted in northern Spain; to capture the incoming Spanish treasure fleet; and to expel the Spanish from Portugal. However, the English navy was repulsed at Corunna, and the invading force failed to capture Lisbon. To cap off a disastrous expedition, a section of the fleet led by Drake was scattered in a storm.

The Spanish became better at defending against English privateer attacks on their treasure fleet, thanks to the use of convoys and improved intelligence networks. As a result, the Spanish were able to ship three times as much silver during the 1590s as they had during the previous decade. In a disastrous attack on the Spanish colonies of Puerto Rico and Panama in 1595–6, the English lost a great many soldiers and ships. Both Francis Drake and John Hawkins died of disease during the expedition. In 1595, a Spanish force under Don Carlos de Mesquita raided Cornwall, striking Penzance and several surrounding villages. The following year, the

English hit back with an attack on Cádiz led by the dashing young Robert Devereux, Earl of Essex. The force sacked the city and destroyed a great number of Spanish ships. At the time, the sack of Cádiz was regarded by the English as a triumph equal to the victory over the Spanish Armada, and Essex became a national hero.

To avenge Cádiz, Philip sent two further armadas to England, in 1596 and 1597. The first was smashed to pieces by storms off northern Spain and the second was scattered by a storm as it approached the English Channel. Philip II was distraught at the news of these failures. In 1597, he fell ill and shut himself away in his palace. After his death in September 1598, his successor Philip III, continued the war but without much enthusiasm. England carried on helping its Dutch allies in their struggle against Spain, and by 1602 there were up to 8,000 English troops fighting in the Netherlands. It would be Elizabeth's successor, James I, who would finally negotiate a peace with Spain with the 1604 Treaty of London.

FRANCE

In 1589, a Protestant, Henry of Navarre, became King Henry IV of France. His succession was opposed by the Catholic League of France, a powerful organization of French Catholics, and by Philip II of Spain. The League controlled Paris, and their armies forced Henry to retreat south. Philip supported the League with his own forces, and Elizabeth feared that the Spanish would take control of the Channel ports. For the first time since the English retreat from Le Havre in 1563, she sent troops into France. An English expeditionary force of 4,000 men, led by Lord Willoughby, was dispatched in late 1589. The English captured a few French towns, but as usual Elizabeth failed to supply sufficient funds and reinforcements. The troops soon ran short of food, and what remained of the army returned to England in 1590. It was a similarly disastrous story for two further military forays in 1591 – the first to Brittany under the command of John Norreys; the second to Rouen under the Earl of Essex. Elizabeth committed another 2,000 troops to France when the Spanish seized Calais in 1596, to little avail. The conflict ended in 1598 with the Peace of Vervins, under which Calais was returned to France.

IRELAND

In 1541, Henry VIII had declared himself king of Ireland. This was an exaggeration of the truth. England controlled the 'Pale', an area around Dublin, and the south. The north and west of the island was predominantly ruled by Gaelic chieftains. Henry tried to win them over by offering them secure titles to their land and a role in government in return for abandoning their law, language and customs in favour of English ways. Progress in this regard was very slow. Under Edward and Mary, efforts were made to speed the process of anglicization through land seizures, imposition of martial law in some places and attempts at colonization. All this proved counter-productive, provoking growing levels of violence against the English as well as outright rebellion.

For Elizabeth, Ireland featured as an 'unwelcome inheritance'. The cost of administering the territory and defending the English communities there had escalated with the recent rise in violence, accounting for 10 per cent of Elizabeth's total revenues. Her first governor, the Earl of Sussex, said he often wished Ireland 'to be sunk in the sea'. Yet withdrawal was unthinkable. Not only would it be a terrible blow to English prestige, but it could also open the way for France or Spain to establish control.

Elizabeth adopted a typically cautious, thrifty and non-confrontational approach to the problem of Ireland – hoping that English ways would spread gradually without any need to force the issue. The policy pleased no one. The Gaelic chieftains remained restless, fearing more land grabs by the English, while the English landowners grew frustrated at Elizabeth's lack of resolve in dealing with Irish violence. The Protestants among them were angered at the Queen's unwillingness to crack down on Catholicism among the Irish. And her desire for a Gaelic translation of the Bible appeared to many to undermine the government's aim of making Ireland English.

Elizabeth did take some proactive steps to strengthen English rule in Ireland. One was 'composition', whereby

Gaelic chieftains were obliged to disband their private armies, and provinces were occupied by English troops under the command of governors, titled Lords President. In return for accepting this state of affairs, the chieftains were exempted from paying taxes and their entitlement to rent from their tenants became legally enforceable. This provoked rebellions in Connaught and Munster, but was successful in other areas such as Thomond. Another policy pursued by Elizabeth was plantations – settlement of areas of Ireland by English people, who would bring with them their language, culture and loyalty to the Crown. This was attempted in east Ulster in 1572–3 and in Munster from 1584. The problem Elizabeth faced here was controlling the actions of the colonists, such as Humphrey Gilbert and Walter Raleigh. They were less interested in spreading English customs than in enriching themselves by provoking locals to futile rebellions and then grabbing their lands. So, while Elizabeth hoped gradually to extend English rule by winning hearts and minds, the colonists preferred conquest by ruthless military domination.

The result was a steady rise in violence and atrocities, especially after 1579 when two strands of dissent – the Gaelic and the Old English Catholics – began to join forces. Thus, between 1579 and 1583, the English rulers faced the Desmond Rebellion in Munster at the same time as an Old English Catholic uprising in the Pale. Elizabeth sent in massive military reinforcements, and both rebellions were brutally suppressed. But this was all just a prelude to the main crisis of Elizabethan rule in Ireland – the Nine Years War – which broke out as a result of attempts to extend English rule across Ulster.

An alliance of Irish clans, known as the Ulster confederacy, came together under the rule of Hugh O'Neill, Earl of Tyrone, and he managed to assemble a well-equipped army that could match Elizabeth's forces in the field. Tyrone inflicted a major defeat on the English at Yellow Ford in 1598, where up to 2,000 English soldiers died. This victory prompted uprisings in Connaught and Munster, and colonists were forced to flee. In 1599 the Earl of Essex was dispatched to Ireland with over 17,000 troops to retake control. Essex attempted first to pacify the south, but he made little progress. Supplies from England failed to arrive, and his expeditions to the north were disastrous failures. Discouraged, Essex returned to England in defiance of Elizabeth's orders.

He was replaced by Charles Blount, Baron Mountjoy, a much more able military commander. Mountjoy established a reliable supply chain, then set about systematically destroying resistance. First he secured the Pale, then he crushed the rebellion in Munster. In 1601, 4,000 Spanish troops landed in Kinsale in support of the rebellion. Mountjoy laid siege to Kinsale, cutting off the harbour entrance so that the Spaniards were trapped inside the town. Tyrone's army marched south to try and join forces with the Spaniards, and in December the

Spanish tried to break out of Kinsale. Mountjoy defeated both the Irish and the Spanish, forcing Tyrone to retreat north and the Spanish to agree a truce and withdraw. Mountjoy then pursued Tyrone north, and forced an unconditional surrender in 1603.

Elizabeth's pacification of Ireland came at a huge cost in lives and money. It was a purely military victory that did nothing to reconcile the Irish to English rule – in fact, the English now enjoyed less indigenous support than they had in 1558. Only military force would maintain Ireland as a colony during the centuries that followed. Elizabeth is reported to have declared that she sent 'wolves, not shepherds, to govern Ireland, for they have left me nothing to govern over but ashes and carcasses'.

CHAPTER TWENTY

Troubled Years

In many ways, the defeat of the Spanish Armada in 1588 marked the high point of Elizabeth's reign. She would never again, within her lifetime, achieve such a level of popularity. The last 15 years of her rule would be dogged by problems at home and abroad. A run of poor harvests during the 1590s, along with the rising costs of the wars in Ireland and the Netherlands, had a damaging effect on the economy. Prices rose and the standard of living fell. New poor laws were passed in 1597 and 1601. These provided a new code for the provision of poor relief in England and Wales, creating a system that would last for the next two hundred years. The impotent poor were to be cared for in an almshouse or poorhouse; the able-bodied poor were to be put to work in a 'house of industry'; and the 'idle poor' and vagrants were to be sent to a 'house of correction' or prison. Pauper children would become apprentices.

POLICY TOWARDS CATHOLICS

Persecution of Catholics, which had been escalating since the early 1580s, became even more intense in the 1590s. Elizabeth did not, as Francis Bacon wrote, like 'to make windows into men's hearts and secret thoughts', yet she expected outward obedience to the law. In 1581, fines for recusancy were increased to 20 pounds – a huge sum – and anyone attempting to convert an English subject to Catholicism was declared guilty of treason. In 1585, a law was passed banning Jesuits from entering the country. They continued to arrive, however. Elizabeth executed some 130 priests during her reign – a large proportion of these in the 1580s and '90s. In 1591, she authorized commissions to interrogate and monitor Catholic families, and in 1593 the Statute of Confinement prohibited recusants from travelling more than 5 miles (8 km) from their home without a licence. Many Catholics hid their faith, holding mass in secret. Wealthy Catholics built priest-holes in their homes. Others chose exile.

BITTER RIVALRY

Elizabeth continued to project an image of serene power, even as her popularity with her subjects declined. Her personal authority remained undiminished, yet during these later years she found it harder to maintain a firm grip over policy. This may have been partly due to the deaths of some of her key advisors, including Dudley in 1588, Walsingham in 1590 and Christopher Hatton in

1591. Only Lord Burghley remained among her original coterie of senior counsellors. And now, for the first time during her reign, factionalism became a feature of court life. A bitter rivalry arose between her latest favourite, the Earl of Essex, on the one hand, and Lord Burghley and his son Robert Cecil on the other.

Essex was first cousin twice removed to the Queen, and the godson of Dudley. He arrived at court in 1584 and she elevated him to the Privy Council in 1587. Elizabeth loved his eloquence and showmanship, and he soon became her favourite. Essex was a warrior by nature and urged a more aggressive foreign policy. His rivals the Cecils were generally more cautious, and the two factions frequently fought for influence over the Queen.

The intense nature of this competition sometimes had fatal consequences. In 1594, Essex charged one of Elizabeth's court physicians, Doctor Roderigo Lopez, with plotting to murder the Queen. This dramatic announcement was actually a ploy to impress the Queen and gain the upper hand in his fight with the Cecils. Lopez, a Portuguese Jew who had converted to Christianity, had lived in London for 35 years and was a highly respected doctor. To Elizabeth's shock, Essex accused Lopez of having contacts with Spanish spies. In fact, Burghley had known about Lopez's Spanish contacts for years, and Lopez had even worked for Burghley as a double agent, helping him to penetrate Spanish spy rings in England. Yet in the febrile atmosphere that now existed at court, Burghley felt he had no choice but to betray Lopez and throw himself behind Essex's efforts to expose the Portuguese doctor's treason. When Essex accused Lopez of having been paid 50,000 crowns by King Philip to murder Elizabeth, the Cecils knew that this was almost certainly untrue. Yet they stood by as Lopez was found guilty of high treason and then hanged, drawn and quartered – the innocent victim of a cynical political game.

Essex charmed Elizabeth and often took liberties with her, for which she always forgave him. During a heated Privy Council debate about Ireland, the Queen cuffed him round the ear after he said something insolent, prompting him to half-draw his sword on her – a treasonable offence for anyone but Essex. She would repeatedly offer him new military commands despite his growing reputation for recklessness and insubordination. In 1597, he and Walter Raleigh led a fleet to the Azores to attack a Spanish battle fleet there. Essex failed to follow orders and the expedition was a failure. Worse, his actions left the homeland dangerously exposed just as Philip of Spain tried to invade with his third Armada. Yet, two years later, Essex was placed in charge of a massive expeditionary force in Ireland. After he deserted his command in Ireland, he was brought before the Council to explain himself. Robert Cecil pressed for Essex to be put on trial.

In June 1600, Essex was convicted of desertion of

duty. He was deprived of public office and placed under house arrest. With his main source of income – a monopoly on sweet wines – withdrawn, Essex's position became desperate. In early 1601, he began to fortify his house on the Strand and gather his followers for a rebellion. On 8 February, he led his supporters into the City of London in an attempt to capture the Queen. Though Essex was popular in the country, few rallied to him that morning. Cecil proclaimed him a traitor, and Crown forces blocked Essex's path, forcing him to withdraw. After they laid siege to his house, Essex surrendered. He was tried and found guilty, and on 25 February he was beheaded on Tower Green – the last person to be executed there. Elizabeth knew that her own misjudgements were partly to blame for Essex's fate. In 1602, a reporter observed: 'Her delight is to sit in the dark, and sometimes with shedding tears to bewail Essex.'

THE SHAKESPEAREAN AGE

From the start of her reign, Elizabeth had been a great patron of the arts. She commissioned famous portrait painters such as Nicholas Hilliard and Marcus Gheeraerts to depict herself and members of her entourage. She also encouraged composers such as Thomas Tallis and William Byrd to create ambitious new works. The Queen's chapel choir of men and boys was greatly admired by foreign visitors. One, who attended a service in the royal chapel at Greenwich, reported, 'In all my travels in France, Italy and Spain, I have never heard the like: a concert of music so excellent and sweet as cannot be expressed.'

William Shakespeare, a playwright who was careful to glorify the House of Tudor.

Yet it was in the area of literature that the Elizabethan era would be best remembered. Among the Queen's courtiers, Sir Philip Sidney and Sir Walter Raleigh were accomplished writers of sonnets, and Elizabeth herself was known to compose poetry. One of the most famous poems of the Tudor age was *The Faerie Queen*, a long allegorical work by Edmund Spenser. At the heart of the piece is the eternally youthful Gloriana, the Faerie Queen, a poetic embodiment of Elizabeth. It found such favour with her that she granted Spenser a pension for life.

Although the 1590s was in many ways a troubled era, it was during this decade that some of the great Elizabethan playwrights came of age, including Christopher Marlowe, Ben Jonson and, of course, William Shakespeare. The Queen adored dramas and pageants, and many plays had their preview at her court, including Shakespeare's *Twelfth Night* in 1601. Elizabeth herself is said to have inspired another Shakespeare play, *The Merry Wives of Windsor*, after she asked the bard to write a play in which her favourite character, Falstaff, fell in love.

THE 'GOLDEN SPEECH'

From the late 1580s, Elizabeth began granting patents to her favoured courtiers as a cost-free system of patronage. Patents gave them the exclusive right to trade in and profit from particular commodities, such as sweet wine, starch and salt. The recipients of these monopolies would be able to fix prices to further enrich themselves.

During the harsh economic conditions of the 1590s, the practice caused widespread resentment, with growing protests from Parliament. In the 1597–8 Parliament, a petition objecting to patents was delivered to the Queen. Elizabeth responded by defending her prerogative 'which is the chiefest flower in her garland and the principall and head pearle in her crowne and dyadem', but promising to review offensive grants 'soe she promiseth to continewe and that they shall all be examined to abide the tryall and true touchstone of the lawe'. Despite her fine words, she continued to issue patents. The resentment increased, culminating in angry scenes in the House of Commons during the Parliament of 1601.

Elizabeth knew that her personal authority was being tested as never before. She was now 68 years old, in failing health and prone to bouts of depression. Yet she rose to the occasion in magnificent style. On 30 November 1601, she invited a deputation of 141 MPs to Whitehall Palace. She spoke to them, professing ignorance of the abuses and disarming them with a speech that none present would ever forget.

There is no jewel, be it of never so rich a price, which I set before this jewel: I mean your love. For I do esteem it more than any treasure of riches; for that we know how to prize, but love and thanks I count invaluable ... I have ever used to set the Last Judgement Day before mine eyes and so to rule as I shall be judged to answer before a higher judge, and now if my kingly bounties have been abused and my grants turned to the hurt of my people contrary to my will and meaning, and if any in authority under me have neglected or perverted what I have committed to them, I hope God will not lay their culps [wrongs] and offenses in my charge. I know the title of a King is a glorious title, but assure yourself that the shining glory of princely authority hath not so dazzled the eyes of our understanding, but that we well know and remember that we also are to yield an account of our actions before the great judge … For myself I was never so much enticed with the glorious name of a King or royal authority of a Queen as delighted that God hath made me his instrument to maintain his truth and glory and to defend his kingdom as I said from peril, dishonour, tyranny and oppression. There will never Queen sit in my seat with more zeal to my country, care to my subjects and that will sooner with willingness venture her life for your good and safety than myself. For it is my desire to live nor reign no longer than my life and reign shall be for your good. And though you have had, and may have, many princes more mighty and wise sitting in this seat, yet you never had, nor shall have, any that will be more careful and loving.

The MPs knew that she was speaking to them almost certainly for the last time. She knew this, too, and asked each of them to kiss her hand before they left. Many MPs were in tears. The oration quickly achieved legendary status. It would become known as Elizabeth's Golden Speech.

DEATH AND LEGACY

In 1598, Elizabeth's most trusted advisor, Lord Burghley, had died. During his final illness, she had sat by his bed and fed him with a spoon. She missed him terribly when he passed away. He was succeeded as chief minister by his son Robert, but the younger Cecil was a cooler, more calculating character, and she would never develop the same rapport with him. Since Elizabeth refused to name a successor, Cecil entered into secret negotiations with James VI of Scotland, who had a strong but not yet officially recognized claim. Cecil coached James in how to win over Elizabeth. His advice worked, and James managed to charm the Queen. She wrote to him: 'So trust I that you will not doubt but that your last letters are so acceptably taken as my thanks cannot be lacking for the same, but yield them to you in grateful sort.'

In September 1602, Elizabeth celebrated her sixty-ninth birthday. She was suffering from rheumatism and her eyesight was failing, but generally she was in good health. That autumn, however, the deaths of several close friends plunged her into deep depression. The death of Catherine Howard, Countess of Nottingham, in February 1603, was a particular blow. At the beginning of March, the Queen took ill with a fever and was unable to sleep. She refused food and began to lose the power of speech. She died in the early hours of 24 March at Richmond Palace.

After five days of lying in state, the Queen's body was carried down the Thames on a torch-lit barge to Westminster Hall. Her funeral, on 28 April, was a grand yet solemn occasion. Thousands lined the streets to pay their respects to 'Good Queen Bess'. In the words of one chronicler, 'there was such a general sighing, groaning and weeping as the like hath not been seen or known in the memory of man'. She was interred in Westminster Abbey in a tomb she shared with her half-sister Mary.

Despite the public outpouring of grief at Elizabeth's death, many looked forward to the reign of James. Yet disillusionment with the Stuart king did not take long to surface. By the 1620s, there was great public nostalgia for Elizabeth, and her reign came to be seen as a golden age.

In many ways it was. For most of her 45-year reign, England enjoyed relative peace and stability. She crafted a religious settlement that strengthened the Church of England and established her kingdom as a Protestant country where Catholics would be tolerated. She understood that monarchs rule by popular consent and always tried to work with Parliament – something her Stuart successors notably failed to do. During her reign, England developed into a significant maritime power and a global trading nation, and under her patronage the nation enjoyed a tremendous flowering of literature and the arts.

Yet critics point to the numerous military failures on land and sea during her reign, and some of this can be blamed on her overly cautious approach to foreign affairs and her failure to support her commanders in the field. Although her forces ultimately prevailed in Ireland, they did so with a brutality that left a stain on her reputation.

These judgements must be weighed against the hand she had been dealt on succeeding to the throne. The England Elizabeth inherited was a weak and divided nation, surrounded by enemies. 'She is only a woman, only mistress of half an island,' remarked an admiring Pope Sixtus V, 'and yet she makes herself feared by Spain, by France, by the Empire, by all.' She instilled a sense of national pride in her people and became a living symbol of resistance to a foreign threat.

Some historians have called her lucky. Elizabeth put her success down to God's protection. '[At a time] when wars and seditions with grievous persecutions have vexed almost all kings and countries round about me, my reign hath been peaceable, and my realm a receptacle to thy afflicted Church. The love of my people hath appeared firm, and the devices of my enemies frustrate.'

EPILOGUE

Of all the families to have ruled England, the Tudors were the most adept at projecting their power and majesty. With such a dubious claim to the throne, they needed to work hard to create an aura of legitimacy. Their badge, the double rose of the rival houses of Lancaster and York, was a masterpiece of propaganda – portraying them as unifiers, bringing peace to a divided, warring kingdom.

Henry VII tried to establish a solid legacy to his family's rule with the building of palaces and chapels. His son, Henry VIII, continued this tradition with an array of magnificent buildings from Hampton Court Palace to King's College Chapel in Cambridge; and paintings portrayed him as a mighty and heroic Renaissance king. Woodcuts showed Henry VIII as supreme head of the Church of England, in direct communication with God, with no need for mediation from priests or pope.

Elizabeth was, in this sense, very much her father's

daughter. In her portraits she looks serene, unmovable and touched by God. In the 'Armada' portrait celebrating her navy's 1588 success against the Spaniards, her right hand rests on a globe of the world while behind her the Spanish fleet is being dashed against the rocks. In the 'Ditchley' portrait of 1592, she has an almost supernatural presence. Behind her, a stormy sky gives way to sunshine. Wearing a bejewelled dress as pale as her face, she stands upon a map of her kingdom, towering above it like a goddess. Even more than her father, Elizabeth managed to inspire both awe and devotion in her subjects.

With their masterful control of image and propaganda, the Tudors were able to impress their subjects and maintain themselves in power for nearly 120 years, surviving all attempts at rebellion. Even during the troubled reigns of Edward VI and Mary I, the government was never seriously challenged. This remarkable dynasty managed to weave a spell of power and splendour that dazzled their people. It continues to dazzle us today.

INDEX

Abergavenny, Lord 55
Alba, Duke of 149
Amicable Grant 51, 54
Anjou, Duke of 139, 141
Anne of Cleves 86–7
ap Rice, John 77
Appeals, Act of 70
Arran, Earl of 142
Arthur, Prince 32, 34, 39
Arundel, Earl of 110, 137
Aske, Robert 80–1
Ayton, Treaty of 31
Babington, Anthony 155, 156, 157
Babington Plot 154–8
Bacon, Francis 174
Ballard, John 154–5, 157
Beaufort, John 11
Beaufort, Margaret 11, 12, 13, 39
Bigod, Sir Francis 81
Blount, Charles 171–2
Boleyn, Anne 59, 61, 65, 68, 70, 71, 72, 84–5, 112
Boleyn, Mary 59
Bond of Association 152–3
Bothwell, Earl of 146–7
Boulogne, Treaty of 107
Bosworth Field, Battle of 10, 12, 14, 15, 16
Brandon, Charles 80, 89
Bryan, Margaret 97
Burghley, Lord 128, 139, 144, 151–3, 158, 161, 175–7, 182
Burgundy, Duke of 28
Byrd, William 177
Cabot, John 33
Cadwaladr (King) 11
Campeggio, Cardinal 63
Catherine of Aragon 32, 37, 40–1, 45, 46–7, 59–65, 67, 68, 71, 112
Catherine of Valois 11
Cecil, Robert 175–6, 182
Cecil, Sir William 128, 139, 144, 151–3, 158, 161, 175, 182
Charles, Archduke 137, 140
Charles V (Holy Roman Emperor) 49, 50, 62, 67, 86, 90, 91, 116
Charles VIII (France) 30
Charles IX (France) 134
Châteauneuf-sur-Cher, Baron de 155–6
Church
        under Edward VI 100–1, 106–7
        under Elizabeth I 128–30, 174
  under Henry VIII 56–8, 66–79, 81–3
  under Mary I 114–15, 120–1
Clement VII (Pope) 62–3, 64, 65, 71
Compton, William 42
Court of Chancery 55, 56
Court of Requests 55
Courtenay, Edward 114, 116
Cranmer, Thomas 70, 71, 85, 86, 88, 89, 101, 115, 121
Cromwell, Thomas 67–8, 69, 70, 76–7, 84, 85, 86–7
Culpeper, Thomas 88
Darnley, Lord 145–7
Davies, John 159
Davison, William 157–8
de la Pole, Edmund 28
de la Pole, John 23
de Vere, John 18
Denmark 32
Dereham, Francis 88
Desmond Rebellion 170
Devereux, Robert 167
Desmond, Earl of 26

Dispensations, Act of 71
Dissolution of the Greater Monasteries, Act for the 81–2
Drake, Francis 136, 162, 166
Dudley, Guildford 108, 115, 117
Dudley, Henry 122
Dudley, John 101, 102, 103–11, 115
Dudley, Robert 138–9, 140, 145, 161–2, 164, 174
Dutch Revolt 134–5
Dynham, Lord 21
Ecclesiastical Appointments and Absolute Restraint of Annates, Act Concerning 71–2
Elisabeth of Valois 107
Edinburgh, Treaty of 144
Edward I 20
Edward III 9
Edward IV 10, 13, 14, 15, 24, 25
Edward V 10, 13, 24, 25
Edward VI 168
    becomes king 95
    birth of 85
    Church affairs 100–1, 106–7
    death of 107–9, 115
    early years 89, 96–7
    minority reign 9, 97–109
Edward, Earl of Warwick 14, 23, 24
Edward of Lancaster 10
Elizabeth I
    birth of 71, 112
    Church affairs 128–30, 174
    coronation 126–8
    court factionalism 175–7
    death of 182–3
    early years 85, 89, 97, 99, 117, 118–19, 125–6
    foreign policy 134–6, 139–41, 159–72
    'Golden Speech' 179–82
    legacy of 183–4
    marriage of 136–41
    and Mary, Queen of Scots 143, 145, 147–9, 151–8
    patron of the arts 177–9
    Poor Laws 130–2, 173
    rebellions 148–9, 170-2
    royal progresses 132–3
    and Spanish Armada 164–5
Elizabeth of York 11, 15–16, 23, 34
enclosures
    under Edward VI 101–2, 105
    under Elizabeth I 131
    under Henry VIII 55–6
Eric of Sweden, Prince 137, 140
Essex, Earl of 171, 175–7
Étaples, Treaty of 30
Faerie Queen, The (Spenser) 179
Ferdinand II (Spain) 32, 45, 46–7, 48
Field of the Cloth of Gold 49–50
finances
    under Henry VII 21–2
    under Henry VIII 51, 52–4
    under Edward VI 105–6
Fisher, John 34
Flodden, Battle of 46
Florence 32
foreign policy
    under Elizabeth I 134–6, 139–41, 159–72
    under Henry VII 29–33
    under Henry VIII 45–51, 90–2
    under Mary I 121–3
Forty–Two Articles 106
Fox, Richard 19, 41, 42
France
    and Edward VI 107
    and Elizabeth I 134, 167–8
    and Henry VII 29
    and Henry VIII 45–51, 90–2
    and Mary I 121–3
Francis I (France) 47, 48–51, 86, 90, 91
Francis II (France) 142–3
Frobisher, Martin 136, 159
Gardiner, Stephen 89, 98, 114, 116
Gheeraerts, Marcus 177
Gifford, George 154, 155–6
Gilbert, Humphrey 136, 170
Greenwich, Treaty of 90–1
Grenville, Richard 136
Gresham, Thomas 106
Grey, Henry 117
Grey, Lady Jane 99, 108–9, 110, 111, 114, 115, 117, 140
Grey, Lady Katherine 140
Grey, Thomas 45
Guinegate, Battle of 46
Hatton, Christopher 174–5
Hawkins, John 136, 166
Hawkins, Richard 136
Henry I, Duke of Guise 152, 155
Henry II (France) 107
Henry IV 9
Henry IV (France) 167
Henry V 9, 11
Henry VI 9, 10, 12, 13
Henry VII 8, 39, 40
    claim to throne 11–12
    coronation 7, 10, 15
    early life 12–13
    finances 21–2
    foreign policy 29–33
    legacy of 33–5
    power consolidation 14–16, 17–22
    rebellions 23–8
    and Thomas Wolsey 42
    Wars of the Roses 10–11, 13–14
Henry VIII 38, 168
    and Anne Boleyn 59, 68, 70, 71, 72, 84–5
    and Anne of Cleves 86–7
    and Catherine of Aragon 32, 40–1, 47, 59–65,

67, 68, 71
and Catherine Howard 87–8
and Catherine Parr 88–9, 92
Church affairs 56–8, 66–79, 81–3
court factionalism 89–90
death of 92–3
descriptions of 37–8
    early reign 41
    early years 39–41
    finances 51, 52–4
    foreign policy 45–51, 90–2
    funeral of 95
    and Jane Seymour 85, 95
    law 54–5, 69
    legacy of 93
    rebellions 51, 79–81
Henry, Prince 47
Herbert, William 13
Heresy Acts 120–1, 129
Heron, Sir John 53
Hilliard, Nicholas 177
Holbein the Younger, Hans 86
Holy League 45, 46–7
Hooper, John 107
Horsey, William 53–4
Howard, Catherine 87–8, 182
Howard, Henry 89–90
Howard, Thomas 18, 21, 46, 81, 86, 87, 89–90, 98, 114, 117, 148–9
Hunne, Richard 53, 56
Innocent VIII (Pope) 32
Ireland 168–72
Isabella I (Spain) 32
James III (Scotland) 30
James IV (Scotland) 26, 30–1, 46
James V (Scotland) 90, 142
James VI/I 146, 147, 167, 182
John of Gaunt 8, 9, 10, 11
Jonson, Ben 179
Julius II (Pope) 45
Julius III (Pope) 120
Justices of the Peace
    under Henry VII 18
Kett, Robert 102
Kett's Rebellion 101–2
Kildare, Earl of 24, 25
King Richard the Third (Shakespeare) 16
Knight, William 63
Latimer, Hugh 121
law
    under Henry VIII 54–5, 69
Layton, Richard 77, 81
Legh, Thomas 77, 81
Leo X (Pope) 46, 48, 66
Lincoln, Earl of 24, 28
Lincolnshire Rising 80
London, Treaty of 48
Lopez, Roderigo 175–6
Louis XII (France) 45, 46, 47
Luther, Martin 69

Margaret of York 24, 26
Marignano, Battle of 47
Marlowe, Christopher 179
Mary I 87, 168, 183
    birth of 60
    Church affairs 114–15, 120–1
    death of 123–4
    early years 71, 89, 97, 106, 112–14
    foreign policy 121–3
    marriage to Philip II 115–19
    rebellions 116–17, 122–3
    and succession to throne 107–10
Mary, Queen of Scots 100, 118
    and Babington Plot 154–8
    and Earl of Bothwell 146–7
    early reign 142–5
    in England 147–8, 151–2
    execution 157–8
    and Lord Darnley 145–7
    rebellions 147
    and Ridolfi Plot 149
    and Rising of the North 148–9
    and Throckmorton Plot 152–4
Mary of Guise 90, 142, 144
Mary Rose 91
Matilda, Empress 60
Maximilian I (Holy Roman Emperor) 28, 32, 45, 46, 48
Medina del Campo, Treaty of 31–2
Medina Sidonia, Duke of 162, 163–4
Mendoza, Bernardino de 152
Merry Wives of Windsor, The (Shakespeare) 179
Mesquita, Don Carlos de 166–7
Michieli, Giovanni 118
monasteries, dissolution of 74–83, 120, 130–1
More, Sir Thomas 67, 70, 72
Moreton, John 18–19, 21–2
Morgan, Thomas 154, 155
Mountjoy, Baron 171–2
Netherlands 32–3, 134–5, 160–2
Nine Years War 171
nobility
    under Henry VII 17–18
Nonsuch, Treaty of 161
Norfolk, Duke of 18, 21, 46, 81, 86, 87, 89–90, 98, 114, 117, 148–9
Norreys, Sir John 166
Northumberland, Duke of 101, 102, 103–11, 115, 148
Northumberland, Earl of 55
O'Neill, Hugh 171–2
Osbeck, John 25
Parliament
    Elizabeth I's 'Golden Speech' 179–82
    under Henry VII 20–1, 22
    under Henry VIII 69–70, 71–2
Parma, Duke of 160, 161, 163
Parr, Catherine 88–9, 92, 97, 99, 125

Paulet, Sir Amias 154
Pavia, Battle of 51
Pembroke, Earl of 110
Perpetual Peace, Treaty of 31
Phelippes, Thomas 156, 157
Philip II (Spain) 115–19, 122, 135, 137, 160, 161, 162, 163, 167–8, 176
Philip III (Spain) 167
Pickering, Sir William 137
Pilgrimage of Grace 79–81
Pinkie Cleugh, Battle of 100
Pius V (Pope) 148
Pole, Reginald 40, 114, 116
Ponet, John 107
Poor Laws 105, 130–2, 173
Praemunire, Statute of 68
Prayer Book Rebellion 101
Raleigh, Walter 136, 170, 179
rebellions
    under Edward VI 101–2
    under Elizabeth I 148–9, 170–2
under Henry VII 23–8
under Henry VIII 51, 79–81
under Mary I 116–17, 122–3
    under Mary, Queen of Scots 147
Repeal, First Statute of 120
Restraint of Appeals, Statute in 70–1
Resumption, Act of 54
Richard III 10, 13, 14, 15
Richard of Shrewsbury 10
Ridley, Nicholas 121
Ridolfi, Roberto 149
Ridolfi Plot 149
Rising of the North 148–9
Rizzio, David 146
Robsart, my 138
Rough Wooing 90–1
Royal Council
    under Henry VII 18–19
Saint-Quentin, Battle of 123
Savoy, Duke of 118
Scotland
    and Edward VI 100, 107
and Henry VII 26, 30–1
    and Henry VIII 46, 90–2
Seymour, Edward 89, 97–8, 99–102, 103–4
Seymour, Jane 85, 95, 97–8
Seymour, John 97
Seymour, Thomas 99–100, 125
Shakespeare, William 16, 179
Sidney, Sir Philip 179
Simnel, Lambert 11, 23–5
Simon, Richard 23–4, 25
Six Articles, Acts of 86, 87, 120
Sixtus V (Pope) 184
Solway Moss, Battle of 90
Somerset, Duke of 89, 97–8, 99–102, 103–4
Spain
    and Elizabeth I 134–6, 160–7, 176
    and Henry VII 31–2

    and Henry VIII 46–7
Spanish Armada 162–5
Spenser, Edmund 179
Stafford, Anne 42
Stafford, Edward 42
Stafford, Thomas 122–3
Stanley, Lord 17
Star Chamber
    under Henry VII 19–20
    under Henry VIII 54–5
Stewart, James 147
Stoke, Battle of 28
Succession, Acts of 71, 85, 88–9
Succession to the Crown Act 72
Suffolk, Duke of 117
Supplication Against the Ordinaries 70
Suppression of Religious Houses Act 78
Supremacy, Acts of 72–3, 120, 130
Sussex, Earl of 169
Swynford, Katherine 11
Tallis, Thomas 177
taxation see finances
Throckmorton, Sir Francis 152
Throckmorton Plot 152–4
Treasons Act 72
Tregonwell, John 77
Tudor, Edmund 11, 12
Tudor, Jasper 12–13, 17
Tudor, Margaret 31, 39, 142, 145
Tudor, Mary 39, 47
Tudor, Owen 11
Tyrone, Earl of 171–2
Uniformity, Acts of 101, 130
Valor Ecclesiasticus 77, 78
Vergil, Polydore 33
Walsingham, Francis 151–3, 154–5, 156, 157, 158, 161, 174
Warbeck, Perkin 25–8, 31
Warham, William 41, 42, 70
Wars of the Roses 9–11, 13–14
Westmoreland, Earl of 122
White, John 123–4
Wolsey, Thomas 41–4, 45–9, 50, 51, 52, 53–8, 62, 63, 67, 74
Wriothesley, Thomas 98
Wyatt, Thomas 116–17
Wyatt's Rebellion 116–17, 126
Wynter, Thomas 57

PICTURE CREDITS